To my Father -

who has taught me to understand
and appreciate the nineteenth century.

iii

1982

MEN, WOMEN, AND THE NOVELIST

Fact and Fiction in the American Novel of the 1870s and 1880s

Teresa Kieniewicz

UNIVERSITY
PRESS OF
AMERICA

Copyright © 1982 by

University Press of America, Inc.

P.O. Box 19101, Washington, D.C. 20036

ISBN (Perfect): 0-8191-2045-6
ISBN (Cloth): 0-8191-2044-8

Library of Congress Catalog Card Number: **81-40727**

INTRODUCTION

> We have no thoughts of our own, no opinions
> of our own; they are transmitted to us,
> trained into us. All that is original in us,
> and therefore fairly creditable or dis-
> creditable to us, can be covered up and
> hidden by the point of a cambric needle.[1]

This fanciful paradox which Mark Twain ascribes to his
Connecticut Yankee sums up the hero's experience in
Arthurian England and his difficulties of introducing
the industrial and democratic system before its time.
With reference to the author this comment seems to
contradict the writer's usual, or at least traditionally
alleged, ambition to be original, to attain novelty -
in thoughts, plots, as well as literary form and
means of expression. It should, however, be taken with
a grain of salt, for Mark Twain's well known love of
a "bon mot" caused him, more than once, to verge away
from absolute truth, even from his personal convictions. Yet Hank Morgan's statement deserves more
attention than if it were just another witty phrase of
Twain's. His reflection on the social and environment
conditioning of human consciousness, which appears
almost a cliche, a commonplace to a twentieth century
reader, carried in 1889 a double load of being a novel
and a highly controversial issue. Such a declaration
of social determinism could well be attacked, disputed,
even resented by the more conservative and respectable
readers. After a hundred years, the debate has lost
its relevance. However, to a scholar, a historian in
particular, Twain's apparently casual remark contains
an unexpected encouragement. The notion that, by and
large, people accept their thoughts and opinions
second-hand, even if phrased as a mere humorous aside,
renders fully legitimate the study of fact and
fiction in his and his contemporaries' works of
imagination. The direct correspondence between a work
of literature and the external, objective world,
accepted not only as obvious but as inevitable,
occured in the nineteenth century novel far more
frequently than today. Therefore novels of the past
century yield to this particular inquiry with greater
ease and better promise of success.

Considering fiction a possible source of historical information, Jerzy Topolski, an eminent historian himself, draws special attention to its peculiar character, its inherent possibilities and limitations. A novel, an encoded message designed to be read and understood, necessarily "functions as a sign because it is a conscious realization of the author's purpose."[2] Besides the general rules of the language, the writer avails himself of other tools: first of all, he has at his disposal the variety of genres, styles, and conventions; his other category consists of non-linguistic elements, particles of content enclosed within his frame. Neither type of signals, which may be called "presenting" and "presented" structures of a literary work, belongs to the language code proper, nor can their significance be fully grasped in the usual process of decoding the message. They demand special attention before their true and often complex meaning becomes evident.

To a scholar examining literature as a historical document both groups of signals are of interest. "The historian should approach a writer as a chronicler fashioning reality described according to his concept or ideal, which means concentrating his attention upon and in a sense telescoping features and character-istics he considers essential."[3] Whatever a novelist may say about his contemporary world, its economy, technology, laws, special stratification, all this is seldom a novelty to a historian who usually knows as much from other sources. He values literature as a document not for what it says straightforwardly but for what it conveys indirectly. He can reach such knowledge only in a careful and detailed examination of all signs, signals, and indications embodied in the work. He must make an inquiry into its author's purpose, his aim in employing a particular form as well as the meaning of its content. Such an explanatory procedure is particularly useful in studying social consciousness, the forces and factors molding human behavior and the hierarchy of values.

Sharing Topolski's standpoint I devote most of my attention to the social consciousness inscribed into late nineteenth century novels. The fictional elements are perhaps the easiest to recognize and point out: characters, situations, plots, fictional biographies or business transactions, newly invented cities and minutely described non-existent houses are all direct and obvious products of the writer's imagination. However probable or commonplace, they remain fictitious. They are essential in creating a make-believe world, hence they are governed, first and foremost, by the laws of composition, selection and artistic effect, and only secondarily by probability and the tangled correlations of actual life.

In distinction to such invention, for this study the term "fact" includes modes of thinking, norms, behavioral patterns. However elusive in themselves, their impact is tangible enough because they direct and control social behavior. They are actually more significant than frequent references to current events which, having once served the novelist as a canvas for his imagined tale, retain this function of a foil in the present study. They complement the view of nineteenth century reality, providing additional evidence and arguments for the discussion. The opposition between fact and fiction thus defined requires, I hope, no further elucidation. Yet in between the two there lies an extensive field of illusions, dreams, ideals, and wishful thinking which properly speaking should be classed neither with the fictitious nor with the real life. However, as long as they operate in social consciousness (i.e. are shared by many) they have the power to influence human actions and emotions or provide motivations and rationalizations - they are also facts. Although they are, one is tempted to say, false. This area in which the borderline between the true and the invented is necessarily blurred, and the problem of distinguishing between the two levels has become central in the present study.

A novel blends all the three types indiscriminately: the more talented a writer, the more perfect their harmony. Consequently, dealing with masterpieces, the task of distinguishing and classifying them requires extensive knowledge and fine discrimination. Between the Civil War and the turn of the century the American novel counts a few masterpieces and a handful of first rate books. The main body, however, tends to be second rate, if not mediocre. Such novels yield easily to the intended analysis, and because of their popularity and appeal to average taste they reflect, I believe, the social consciousness of the age with fair adequacy.

In my effort to attain a more complete understanding of the age and its frame of mind, I devoted much energy attempting to discern the elements introduced into the novel on purpose - willingly and consciously - from those that found their way into fiction unintentionally (and are truer for the very fact of "slipping" into the text). It should be stressed at this point that the book does not aim at construing a model of how social consciousness functions.

The present study aims not so much at distinguishing or separating fact from fiction as it hopes to describe a fragment of American reality. Hence, much attention is given to correlations between various social and economic processes which, occurring at the same time, fed on one another. As often as not, they are traced to common causes. Conversely, a single change frequently evoked different responses in various spheres of public life. My fragmentary interpretation attempts to order my vision of American society in the last quarter of the nineteenth century, bringing forth a unity underlying many chaotic and confused experiences of the age - hopefully without narrowing or oversimplifying the perspective. Numerous value studies on American social history, economy, and culture in this period employ highly diverse terminology. Each focusses on a specific, closely analysed aspect so that, when taken together, they give an impression which appears to me incorrect. The diverse processes altering American society after the Civil War are essentially all aspects of the same complex reality. In other words, it seems to me, we are dealing with basically one process, not many. Their apparent multiplicity results on the one hand from focusing on smaller fragments, and from lack of agreement about terminology on the other. In the final analysis social structure, I believe, is so closely knit that a shift or change in any one aspect affects the entire fabric.

The book is divided into three parts corresponding to the main components of the title - men, women, and the novelist. Their sequence mirrors the progress of my research and reflection on the late nineteenth century novel and society. Beginning with detailed analysis of chosen novels in parts one and

4

two, I shift to more general considerations and conclusions in part three. The crucial argument which closes the discussion decided both the selection of material and its arrangement. The position of a novelist in society precedes his writing and indirectly shapes his fiction. It molds his views, ideas, and idiosyncrasies. By. drawing attention to them, I hope to clarify the resulting vision of society and the novelist's place in it. Thus, the first two parts are factual while the third, of a more general character, encloses such opinions and arguments drawn from secondary sources that support my point.

Among the great variety of books dealing with the post-CivilWar America, monographs seem to outnumber attempts at a synthesis. This tendency is most noticeable in literary criticism: there is an abundance of studies on individual authors while those attempting to interpret literature of the entire period are far less numerous. Of these, Jay Martin's The Harvest of Change (1967), offering a wealth of literary and non-literary information, provided the first interest and incentive. Literature dealing with success suffers no shortage of studies and analysis; the interest in fiction by and for women is of a comparatively recent date and unfortunately it is often biased by a too narrow point of view. I remain greatly indebted to three authors - Rex Burns (Success in America: the Yeoman Dream and Industrial Revolution, 1976), Ann Douglas (The Feminization of American Culture, 1978) and Stow Person (The Decline of American Gentility, 1973). The three prompted the germ of my idea about the polarization of American society and the consequent dilemma of the novelists. I sought to develop and confirm it through fairly diverse, though obviously not comprehensive, reading in social history.

The primary sources can be divided into three large groups: novels, literary magazines, and didactic literature. Among about forty chosen novels of the period, more than twenty are of the popular kind, chiefly mediocre, with Horatio Alger at the very bottom. The rest include ten of true literary merit (James, Howells, Chopin, Twain, Wharton) as well as another ten of lesser talent and importance: DeForest, Rebecca H. Davis, Kirkland,

5

John Hay, Fuller, C. D. Warner, whose books are seldom
remembered or read today except by specialists.
Selecting somewhat arbitrarily novels focused on the
principal social problems of the day - success,
corporations, capital-labor relations, graft,
marriage and society life - I necessarily exclude
those dealing with other topics: local color, humor,
adventure etc. At the same time I found it
advisable to eliminate important and influential
writers of the younger generation, Crane and Norris
among them, who, continuing in this literary
tradition, were nevertheless writing from a different
standpoint. Their premises and assumptions tend to
be more often aggressive or assertive than defensive.
In the following discussion I approach the chosen
authors as if they composed a separate social or
professional group. I am fully aware of numerous
differences in their social affiliations, family
backgrounds, financial means, jobs, and writing
careers. Nevertheless they all belonged to the
middle class, broadly understood, and they all were
writers. The value system and life experience they all
shared as a generation, as citizens as well as
novelists, seem to justify grouping them together.
Nor do I perceive any significant difference between
novels written by men and women - as writers.

Three literary magazines, The Atlantic (1868-1880),
The Century (1880-90), and Galaxy (1866-1878), served
me as a guide to interests, opinions, controversies
and literary tastes prevailing among middle and upper-
middle class readers of the two decades. Magazine
short stories seem to reflect the mood and attitudes
of the day with greater immediacy than novels; they
are usually explicit in their message and respond
directly to the readers' expectations. At the same
time the magazines offered access to serious and
intelligent journalism, respectable in tone and
responsible in opinions. Compared with views
enclosed in fiction it reveals a remarkable discrepancy in the respective attitudes and standpoints.

Finally I consulted some of the abundant
didactic literature of the period: guidebooks of
self-help and success for young men and comparable
tracts for girls. The latter outline the proper ways
to get married and secure family happiness. Etiquette
books which enjoyed tremendous popularity at the
time contain advice on social conduct; they are

6

addressed primarily, though not exclusively, to women.

The title limits my considerations to the two decades of the 1870s and 1880s, although I actually move fairly freely from the end of the Civil War to the turn of the century. A further exception is made for Edith Wharton: I wished to include The Age of Innocence because it describes the New York elite of the 1870s in retrospect. Due to the temporal and emotional distance both the structure and character of this confined world appear with greater lucidity.

There is actually little consensus among historians concerning dates. Many regard the Civil War as a dividing point and extend the nineteenth century until World War I; others argue that the years between 1840 and 1890 should be taken as a separate unit - the time of America's growth to industrial maturity. Both views of American history can be documented convincingly. Emphasizing unity rather than divisions I perceive the crucial problems of the twenty years under discussion as resulting from changes and processes initiated some thirty or forty years earlier. Nevertheless, the Civil War helped to speed them up and rendered the shift from the old to the new more apparent to the contemporary.

I owe gratitude and thanks to the American Council of Learned Societies for the grant which enabled me to conduct research for this work in the United States, and also to Robert Regan who advised and encouraged me in the initial stage with patience and good humor. I fully recognize my debt to friends and superiors at Institute of English, Warsaw University for their good-will and general helpfulness. I also thank my friends - Orm Øverland for his unfailing interest, long discussions and criticism, and Timothy Wiles for his generous, invaluable help in editing and publishing this book.

Notes

[1] Mark Twain, *A Connecticut Yankee in King Arthur's Court*, New York, 1930), p. 150.

[2] Jerzy Topolski, "Problemy metodologiczne żrodel literackich w badaniu historycznym," a paper read at IBL PAN colloquium, Warsaw, December 1976. Translation mine.

[3] *Ibid*.

Part One

MEN

Success ideal

Among numerous factors shaping American reality
in the last quarter of the nineteenth century,
business was perhaps the most clearly perceived to
be so by contemporary minds. In all ranks of
society people directly experienced such consequences
of the industrial revolution as the rise of new
industries, the growth of the transcontinental
railroad network, the inflow of immigrants, and
the consolidation of capital and production in
trusts and monopolies. They were no less keenly
aware of the closing of the Western frontier, steady
growth of labor movement, corruption of the legislatures and courts as well as the lack of federal or
state control over the economy. Nevertheless, the
economic doctrines of capitalism, free competition
and laissez faire prevailed in their convictions
about the correct ways of doing business. The term
itself was associated first of all with industry and
commerce; it came to denote financial operations only
gradually during the 1870s - a clear indication of
the increasing importance of capital, the stock
exchange, and banking. Regardless of its particular
form business shaped to a large extent the social
consciousness of the day: success in business became
the dominant incentive of American society.

The concept was by no means new. It formed a
part of the Puritan heritage supported and justified
by the Protestant ethic; it was further popularized
by Benjamin Franklin. Ever since Poor Richard's
Almanac and Autobiography Franklin's model of
success held remarkable appeal for the American
public. In the course of the nineteenth century it
was promoted by such established institutions as
school and church while being spread by journalists
and numerous writers of fiction.

The so-called success literature covers a
considerable variety of books, the most numerous
being handbooks of self-help containing detailed

advice on the right ways and means of making a
fortune.[1] Beteen 1865 and 1900 they were addressed
to young success seeking readers of the lower socio-
economic classes. The model that emerges from them
outlines the ideal course of action for a male youth
between the age of ten and twenty-five. Its initial
assumption is that "success is not accidental but a
subject to fixed rules,"[2] therefore it is accessible
to everybody regardless of external circumstances.
Many writers argue that humble origin and limited
financial means prepare a boy better for the life-
long struggle for success than a comfortable middle
class family background.

        Coming from a poor but honest family in a rural
or small town environment, the boy starts his
career with health, wholesome habits of living and
thinking, an uncorrupted soul, and high ambition as
his only capital. His formal education is limited
to the three "R"s (reading, writing, and 'rithmetic)
which should then be broadened through systematic
self-tuition in all kinds of useful, practical
knowledge. Many authors insist that a good habit
of reading everything except novels (which, as
L. U. Reavis stresses, "breed laziness and idle
thinking"[3]) can easily be equivalent to a university
education. In choosing his first employment the model
boy is usually advised to try opportunities in the
immediate neighborhood before venturing into the
unknown. Cities may offer more attractive jobs but
their influence is often insidious and corrupt.[4]
He begins his apprenticeship as a general helper in
a store or an office, and gains gradual initiation
into his trade while winning the recognition and
trust of his superiors. Never shirking or despising
manual tasks as ones beneath his dignity, he aims to
attain independence or ownership, partnership, or at
least management. Through years of prompt and
faithful service the success winner works steadily
for the benefit of his employer, seeks responsibilities, and acquires knowledge and skills beyond
his immediate duties. His efforts are directed at
becoming indispensable in his employment on the one
hand and constant self-improvement on the other.

        Self-instruction, health, and clean living are
essential, but success depends, as all experts in
the field agree, totally and exclusively upon

character. The list of required virtues runs as
follows:

- honesty and integrity,
- self-respect and self-reliance,
- industry,
- resolution, perseverance, patience,
- reliability, punctuality, accuracy,
- politeness and cheer,
- temperance, cleanliness, simple living, healthy
  habits,
- modesty and frugality.

Each virtue has an importance of its own, each
bears its proper fruits; the example of men of wealth
who, when young, followed the prescribed code
(Andrew Carnegie, the millionaire without flaw being
the prime authority here) was considered definitive.

        The list of cardinal sins was equally uniform.
The most deadly of all is alcohol which ruins
physical and moral health; next in line stands
gambling which "breeds on laziness and cupidity,
... ruins character for it means getting something
for nothing."[5] Smoking leads to laziness if nothing
worse; novels, theatre, skating and the waltz are
banned in the name of purity.

        In the two decades following the Civil War
success was usually identified with big money.
However, with economic conditions increasingly
tough and business competition ruthless, the handbooks of self-help begin to define success as
different from mere accumulation of wealth. Already
in the mid 1880s spiritual values - rectitude, virtue,
esteem - are viewed as desirable in equal measure to
fortune. Before the century was over they were presented as the only praise-worthy goal, financial
gains being a pleasant supplement to moral
satisfaction.[6] The shift in emphasis reflects the
ups and downs of the American economy. Such changes
in interpretation, however, were infrequent. The body
of success literature continued to promote the
model of the past as if unaware of changes in business
practice. Most guidebooks of self-help envisioned
prospects of an independent, comparatively small,
personally managed enterprise which actually had
little chance to prosper after the panic of 1873 and
the following depression.

11

The conditions created by the Civil War were exceptionally favorable for success. Technical inventions, newly discovered resources, improved manufacturing and organization multiplied opportunities for achievement for young men of bold initiative and courage who reached manhood and were entering careers in mid-1860s.[7] The lot of a handful of lucky individuals came to be regarded as a universal law. Depression, slack business, and periodical panics failed to influence it because these events were considered either transitory difficulties or the consequences of irresponsible stock exchange machinations.

The ideal "from rags to riches" derived further power of conviction from biographies and memoirs; in fact, these bear all the characteristics of a didactic treatise and were frequently written and read in the same frame of mind as the guidebooks of self-help. Leo Lowenthal observes that

> this unbroken confidence in the opportunities open to every individual serves as the Leitmotive of the biographies. To a very large extent they are to be looked upon as examples of success which can be imitated. These life stories are really intended to be educational models. They are written - at least ideologically - for someone who next day may try to emulate the man whom he has just envied.[9]

The guidebooks to success as well as biographies are openly didactic - they indicate ways and means, they point out things that must be done and achieved before one wins the prize. Their authors took some inspiration directly from life, accepting as sufficiently convincing the evidence of poor youngsters who, by adhering faithfully to the code, reached the very top positions. At the same time they made use of any and every argument which conceivably might support their point, drawing on Christian teaching, Christian Science, social Darwinism, phrenology, New Thought, evolution - as personal conviction directed. It was the novelist's task to test the doctrine, i.e., to show it operating successfully in an imaginary but probable reality of fiction. It seems that the task was willingly undertaken, for the

12

theme of success is seldom absent from popular as well as serious fiction of the time.

Horatio Alger is known for serial production of mediocre novels perhaps more often referred to than read to-day. Each book, whether from the "Ragged Dick" or "Luck and Pluck" series, can serve as a case study, with the hero starting at the very bottom, grasping instinctively the rules of success, and comfortably settled in the middle ranks of society by the end of the novel. The careers Alger outlines for his heroes vary but little; they are, with few exceptions, confined to commerce. Alger's ideal of business methods and business relations is already outdated - it is the eighteenth century mercantile house. J. G. Cawelti suggests that this evoking of the economic life of an earlier period was, in fact, an attempt at "a reassertion of the values of a by-gone era."[10] The hero works hard, is honest and virtuous, but as often as not his reward is a result of good luck, much in the manner of the folk hero who marries the princess and inherits the kingdom. Or he plays a Cinderella helped through numerous trials by the timely appearances of a fairy godmother disguised as a benevolent merchant. Thus, he seldom earns his fortune by actual work; much more frequently he finds it or is given one at the end of an incredible plot. The element of luck, so persistent in Alger stories, was his own contribution to the success myth; neither the Protestant ethic nor contemporary guide-books admitted its importance.

However tedious in their lengthy, moralizing comments on the characters' decisions, thoughts and deeds, Alger's books enjoyed a tremendous popularity. They sold well enough in his life time; James D. Hart claims that toward the end of the century they "sold millions upon millions of copies to be given to children who generally prefered to think of success in terms of dime-novel heroics."[11] His plots contained the necessary amount of adventure and suspense to hold his unsophisticated readers' attention, and their details about daily life in New York City provided additional excitement to many who still believed the metropolis the nest of evil, wickedness and corruption. Written primarily for a didactic purpose, Horatio Alger novels were a curious mixture of fairy tale and adventure which offered his juvenile

public a romantic escape from their daily struggle
for success.

Success literature must have been wide-spread
indeed and its influence next to omnipresent to
provoke Mark Twain. His "Story of the Good Little
Boy Who Did Not Prosper" (first published in Galaxy,
May 1870) is unequalled in its brilliant attempt to
laugh the idea out of existence. All his life the
good little boy follows diligently all the precepts
taught by Sunday School books concerning ways to sure
and quick success. He is deeply disturbed when his
good deeds go by unnoticed and unrewarded or his
faith and trust are abused.

> He believed in the good little boys. . .
> They always had a good time; and the bad
> little boys had the broken legs, but in
> his case there was a screw loose some-
> where, and it all happened the other
> way. . . Nothing ever came out according
> to the authorities with him . . . His
> case was truly remarkable.[12]

Like many of Mark Twain's readers and admirers his
hero never perceives the distinction between the
realm of dreams, wishful thinking, and actuality.
Therefore, he never learns to deal with reality, to
compromise and to win, but ends in failure. The
dream, however, proved singularly persistent; Twain's
bitter but laughable parody did not undermine the
general faith in a ready and easy way to establish
true success.

Among numerous magazine short stories only one,
"Boring for Oil" (The Atlantic, June 1875) reads like
a typical success tale. In spite of difficulties and
his neighbors' jeers William Maxwell perseveres in
drilling for oil on his farm until the venture proves
successful beyond expectations. However, before
the story closes with a fabulous fortune and a fairy
tale formula "they lived happily ever after," the
author (signed B. W.) gives it an ironic twist. The
oil catches fire, Maxwell is killed, the family ruined
while the profitable oil fields pass into the hands
of a large concern. The dream does not come true
but brings disaster. In the 1870s, as the movement
toward the monopoly system was altering economic and
social structures, the chances of an individual and

14

independent business success were thus put to question.

Other contributors to serious literary magazines
like Galaxy, The Atlantic, and The Century found, it
seems, the topic of business success unconvenial, or
perhaps the editors were not really interested in the
subject. The three magazines published a considerable
amount of fiction - at least one serialized novel,
often two, plus two or three short stories in each
issue. In compliance with the prevailing taste these
works focused on sentiment, their plots invariably
leading to marriage or reunion. The concept of
success is nevertheless very much present in the
magazine fiction, though its expression is more
often implicit than explicit. It appears frequently
as a subplot, a background detail, or betrays its
presence in the characteristic rhetoric. Henry W.
Sedley makes a deliberate use of it in "Our Ranch
at Zion" (Galaxy, September 1876). Its young narrator
declares: "I'm young and ambitious and have come out
here to make money . . . and at home . . . we're all
poor as church mice," only to hear a popular cliche in
an ironic response: "Surely . . . poor but honest,
and the sole support of his widdered mother and
seven small brothers and sisters."[13] The less skillful writers voice their opinions in a direct
authorial commentary;[14] more accomplished ones, like
Henry James, put the judgment into the mouth of one
of the characters.

> . . . you're a failure! . . . Don't talk
> about chances. Don't talk about fair
> starts and foul starts . . . it lies
> neither in one's start to make one a
> success, nor in anything one's brother
> can do or can undo. It lies in one's
> will! You . . . had none.[15]

A more direct emphasis, effective perhaps with the
juvenile audience, would be misplaced in a literary
magazine.

Successful characters presented in these
short stories differ considerably from the model
promoted by the guidebooks of self-help. Several
elements of primary importance to it, such as the
boy's formative years, the beneficial influence of
home, and his early apprenticeship, never enter
the plot except as an occasional aside. However,

their fundamental identity with it remains unmistakable. The main character is, understandably, not a teenage boy but a handsome, likeable man in his twenties - old enough to participate in adult life, to share its difficulties and responsibilities, but still with his financial and sentimental fortune yet to make. He is presented as a free agent, unrestricted and unconditioned by the environment and therefore fully responsible for his actions. The writers seem to share the prevailing view, declaring that success depends solely on a man's character, as if unaware of the Darwinian or Spencerian concept of society.

While success and failure are measured by prosperity and financial gain, it remains clear that the writers considered this external evidence of secondary importance. Their evaluations assess moral qualities as the first and foremost standard of achievement. Much like in the guidebooks of self-help, in the magazine fiction, references to sins against success appear as frequently as the presentation of the necessary virtues. Greed for large and quick gains with the consequent or accompanying gambling fever is inimical to success in the same way as dishonesty, laziness, or other deficiences in character.[16]

To Henry James, the problem of amassing money is of less immediate interest, but when he touches upon it he treats it with subtlety. According to the letter of the success code, Edgar in "Guest's Confession" (The Atlantic, October 1872) is a model of honesty and prudence. In his own eyes, his business conduct is exemplary, unblemished by fraud or speculation. Hence, his sense of self-righteousness seems fully justified. Yet James casts him in the role of a villain pitted against Mr. Guest who sinned by using entrusted money for speculation. Guest's guilt is undisputable, but he is weak, not wicked. For all the outward show of virtue, Edgar is more dangerous. His power is destructive because it serves neither justice nor mercy but feeds his own insatiable greed and pride. For his crime of humiliating a fellow man, James finds no easy or ready pardon.

Dealing with the question of success or business, the fiction writers seldom take a definitely negative stand. The prevailing attitude is one of concern, not criticism. They neither reject nor condemn the business mentality of their time. Rather they perceive deficiencies and limitations inherent in the popular code of success achievement. Most frequently, perhaps, they are concerned that the incessant drive to action leaves little, if any, leisure for other than pecuniary interests. To their perception, the constant preoccupation with money is the main cause for American society remaining culturally and intellectually impoverished. Comments and complaints voiced by the female characters who sense themselves neglected by men striving for success are frequent and seem characteristic.

William Dean Howells, a realist and a social critic, is interested in but one aspect of success - the consequences a spectacular financial gain may have for an individual psyche. The problem constitutes the central axis of events in The Rise of Silas Lapham (1885); Howells uses it again in A Hazard of New Fortunes (1890) for a secondary, though not marginal plot. The external realities of his contemporary America - rapid industrialization, urbanization, and the growth of monopolies - seldom become the direct object of his criticism because, taken by themselves, they are morally neutral. Without accepting the new social philosophy (or its catch phrases like natural laws, impersonal forces, selection, evolution) Howells is well aware how one's course of action is constantly modified in and by social intercourse. Thus, neither of his two successful characters, Silas Lapham and Jacob Dryfoos in The Rise of Silas Lapham and A Hazard of New Fortunes respectively, is truly a self-made man. The author points out that Dryfoos is pushed to speculation by his ambitious daughters who force him to sell the family farm. In New York, he sponsors the literary magazine to distract Conrad from the ministry; finally he retires from business crushed by his son's death. Similarly, Mrs. Lapham's rigid righteousness and Roger's unscrupulous manipulation mold Silas's decisions. This dependence, Howells makes it clear, is reciprocal: Lapham's and Dryfoos's actions shape the lives of their families and associates.

In a stereotypical success story the fundamental change in the hero's fortune is brought about by an apparently insignificant event. Horatio Alger's

17

novels invariably abound in such incidents. Narrating
the story of Silas Lapham, Howells makes far subtler
use of the device. From the initial discovery of the
mineral paint deposits until the final option of
saving his business by selling the mills, Lapham's
life is greatly shaped by chance. Yet particular
incidents, including the crucial though accidental
meeting with Rogers, seem almost commonplace. At
the time they happen their implications remain unclear,
only to be revealed later. Their importance for
advancing the plot is consciously obliterated in order
to enhance their psychological impact. By focusing on
the dramatic consequences of commonplace events,
Howells displays the complexity of human experience.
The impact of the environment, however, is never
offered as an excuse for his characters' misconduct.
Howells adheres to the older view of society as
composed of conscious and rational individuals,
free in their choices and therefore morally
responsible. Though he presents them operating in,
altering and being altered by, a complex social framework, he seems to subscribe, on a deeper level, to
the fundamental creed of individualism.

The Rise of Silas Lapham opens with an interview.
The main character's simple, slightly naive story,
told with a touching sense of dignity and satisfaction,
is turned by the young Boston journalist into a
classical rise from rags to riches.

> His early life, its poverty and hard-
> ships, sweetened . . . by the
> recollections of a devoted mother and
> father . . . His life affords an
> example of single-minded application
> and unwavering perseverence which our
> young business men would do well to
> emulate.[17]

The familiar rhetoric as well as choice of details
are employed with skill. Furthermore, Howell's
handling of the plot enforces the impression that this
resemblance was consciously planned; his aim was to
evoke clear and definite associations between his
story and the popular ideal.

Howell's two characters, Lapham and Dryfoos, fit
the model of a poor country youth who attains
prosperity to the letter. In both cases an unexpected

18

discovery of valuable mineral deposits on the family
farm becomes the turning point in life. They abandon
farming for business and make their fortune. Yet
Howells is not interested in the process of
accumulating wealth. His novels take up the story
only when money-making becomes fully accomplished.

In A Hazard of New Fortunes the fabulous fortune
proves destructive to Dryfoos not because of any evil
inherent in money or in the fact of possessing it.
The way he gained his millions through speculation
was impure.

> . . . his moral decay began with his
> perception of his opportunity of making
> money quickly and abundantly . . .
> The money he had already made without
> effort and without merit bred its unholy
> self-love in him, he began to honor
> money, especially money that had been
> won suddenly and in great sums; for
> money that had been earned painfully,
> slowly, and in little amounts he had
> only pity and contempt.[18]

Thus Dryfoos has broken the essential rule of honest
success as a well-earned reward for years of hard
work and saving. He commits yet another sin by
spending his millions on personal extravagancies or his
daughters' frivolities instead of using them for the
benefit of society.

His moral degradation results from his mistaken
conviction that money can buy everything. A sense of
power to control the lives of those who depend on him
financially turns him into a tyrant indifferent to the
wishes and needs of his family. By the same right he
feels authorized to exercise control over the
political views of his employees.

> He's come to despise a great many things
> that he once respected. . . he must have
> undergone a moral deterioration, an
> atrophy of generous instincts. . .[19]

In Howells's view Dryfoos fails because he yields to
the corrupting influence of riches; examining his
case, the experts on success-making would concentrate
perhaps on different aspects but their verdict would

19

be the same.

The Rise of Silas Lapham analyses the problem in greater detail, hence the correspondence with popular views is more evident. Lapham's moral dilemma concerns the subtle sphere of motivation of human action. Buying out a partner is no crime, yet Lapham's conscience is not easy. His wife's charge strikes painfully home:

> you had made your paint your god, and you couldn't bear to let anybody share in its blessing. . . You took an advantage![20]

Dealing with Rogers, Lapham acted legally but dishonorably because motivated by greed and selfishness. This impurity of intention renders him a helpless prey to Rogers's later machinations. With skill and ruthlessness, he works on Lapham's sense of guilt, drawing him to imprudent action.

> I wanted to make it up to you, if you felt anyways badly used. And you took advantage of it. You've got money out of me. . .[21]

The list of Lapham's faults is long. He speculates, lends money without adequate securities, and begins construction of a new house when the market is dull, thus undermining his financial position. He has a chance of saving his business by taking advantage of someone's trust and ignorance. Ironically enough, Howells makes him follow the best rules of the success game and fail. Lapham goes bankrupt. In the struggle he reaches spiritual maturity and moral uprightness:

> but if they were victories of any sort he bore them with the patience of defeat.[22]

In both novels Howells avails himself of popular concepts, stock situations and the idiom which success literature had made well familiar to the general public. He employs them consciously and with masterly skill to render the contrast between material and human values all the more striking. His judgment upon Silas Lapham is unequivocal: his moral choice is the one that America has to face and solve, hopefully for a better future.

Admittedly, W. D. Howells should not be placed in the same class with Horatio Alger, Orion Sweet Harden and other "authorities" on success. He shares more with Edward Everett Hale, Robert Grant, T. B. Aldrich, Frank Stockton and others who contributed regularly to The Atlantic of which he was then the editor, or to other magazines of the kind. In spite of differences in artistic quality, their prose is marked, in varying degrees, by the influence of the success ideal. It serves writers of various ranks and tastes as a handy frame of reference, it provides a wealth of cliched phrases, stereotypical characters and situations, and its basic concepts are used to motivate such facts as personal achievement or bankruptcy. We may safely infer from the frequency of its appearance in fiction that it constituted a prominent, recognizable element in the American society of the time. The resemblances can be easily accounted for as being due to the common fund of experience and vocabulary. The statement, however unsatisfactory, is nevertheless true.

To the nineteenth century prose writers the success ideal was a phenomenon which could hardly be ignored. While their interest was directed primarily to sentiment, manners, or ethics, they recorded the behavior of their fictional characters - for the most part their own contemporaries, average Americans of the 1870s and 1880s. To a considerable extent their popularity depended upon their ability to win their reader's consent to the credibility of the story and his acceptance of the author's argument and point of view. When dealing with contemporary affairs it was particularly important to meet the reader's idea of the probable, and thus convince him of the truth or feasibility of the fictional characters and turns of the plot. The familiar setting, convincing mode of behavior, idiom of speech, and range of professed values and ideas served as tools and material for building recognizable characters and situations.[23]

The frequent allusions to the familiar success code serve many a writer as an easily identifiable frame of reference, introduced to enhance the illusion of the writer's veracity. As such, the success ideal with its characteristic rhetoric appears not as a proposition to be supported, disproved, or argued about. Actually, the writer's personal attitude toward the popular ideal loses much significance; as often as not its function was one of a tool employed to build up a credible, realistic, though fictional world.

Thus, on the level of the novelistic technique, the success ideal offers a master key to understanding the social scene of the later nineteenth century. Its other function, in the processes of socialization, is equally important. Analysing the relation between fact and fiction, Joan Rockwell ascribes special significance to the social role of literature:

> Fiction is not only a representation of social reality, but also paradoxically an important element in social change. It plays a large part in the socialization of infants, in the expression of official norms such as law and religion, in the conduct of politics, and in the less easily definable but basic areas such as norms, values, and personal and inter-personal behaviour.[24]

Through the very repetition, fiction ingrains such patterns of thought, argument, and behavior that are socially desirable. Its persuasive power lies first of all in its appeal to the reader's emotions and imagination.

By its very nature literature bears a normative character. Whether a novelist accepts the notion or denies it, his attitude toward his fictional characters and their fate influences his reading public and molds their notion of correct, acceptable behavior. When an industrious, sober, and generally lovable hero wins his fortune, his lot is in perfect accordance not with the actual, everyday experience of the reader but with his firm conviction that it should be so.

Response to social reality

Subscribing on the whole to American individualism, the novelists took a broader than merely

22

personal view of the world; they were acutely aware
of manifold currents and forces which were altering
all aspects of their daily lives. While the sense
of change was, it seems, the dominant experience,
responses to it were anything but uniform: they
ranged from whole-hearted approval to fundamental
repudiation. The restless, energetic post-Civil War
generation found it easy enough to accommodate technical inventions[25] and industrial improvements that
obviously increased public safety, comfort, and
efficiency. The magic term "progress" expressed
unconditional approval. The other side of the
coin - Black Friday (1869), railroad strike (1877),
Haymarket riots (1886), or the Homestead Steel
strike (1892) - was too confusing to come to terms
with. The social turmoil Americans witnessed and
participated in seemed both incomprehensible and
incompatible with progress. It required a conscious
effort to analyze and rationalize about the disturbing phenomena of the contemporary life before
any remedy could be suggested: the effort which
frequently took the shape of a novel.

Every area of public life was subjected to
scrutiny. Problems were closely observed,
diagnosed, and ways of improvement provided.
Many novelists used the novel form as the most
efficient tool to awake the mass public to immediate
social evils, to win support for some suggested
reform, finally to stir readers to action. The
novel could bring abstract ideas home to unsophisticated people who would never follow more
intellectual arguments of serious journalism,
economic tracts or sociological essays. It could
plead the cause all the more effectively because it
provided rational arguments while reinforcing the
message by its strong emotional and imaginative
appeal. Many novelists discovered in the <u>roman à thèse</u>
the surest way to a financially gratifying popularity
and used their skill to advocate the chosen "cause"
with a genuine sense of serving (efficiently!) the
public as well as personal interests best.

The growing awareness of social evils and abuses
converged with the all-American insistence on
improvement to produce something like a crusading
zeal for reform in all possible spheres: temperance
movements, purity crusades, co-op systems, profit-
sharing, single-tax, labor organizations, female

23

emancipation, dress reform - to name but some of the more important. Commenting how much propaganda was then cast in the form of fiction, James D. Hart quotes samples of contemporary opinions.

> A caustic journalist inquired, "Do you wish to instruct, to convince, to please? Write a novel! Have you a system of religion or politics or manners or social life to inculcate? Write a novel!" So many earnest souls took his advice that the historian Motley (himself an unsuccessful novelist) grumbled, "Certainly the world should be reformed, but not entirely by novel writers.[26]

In the large field of industry and business the question of capital-labor relations attracted most attention. New technology enforced radical changes in industrial production: machine operating required fewer and less skilled hands; at the same time it allowed mass production by employing thousands of workers who were as exchangable as cogs and bolts in the machinery they were running. Under the spreading monopoly system the workers' life, both inside the shop and at home, was increasingly if indirectly controlled. With industry expanding in all directions, the opportunities for the working class were, paradoxically enough, narrowing down. Their life was becoming regimented. The capitalist controlled the hours, wages, safety, and working conditions; furthermore, his influence frequently extended to housing, stores and their supplies and prices, occasionally even to amusements. The factory system limited effectively the possibilities of advancement since it offered little chance of self-improvement in body or mind, of acquiring skills necessary for more complex tasks, or of undertaking responsibilities outside one's immediate duty. Thus, the gap between the exploiters and the exploited was widening rapidly, with accumulated wealth on the one hand and dire poverty on the other, combinations and alliances among producers set against unorganized labor. The grinding exploitation, worsened by reoccurring depressions, created tensions and conflicts which were bound to break out in violence. These may seem to us an inevitable by-product of capitalism, but to the nineteenth century public the

24

news of class hatred, violent clashes, riots, general warfare, and enmity was still shocking. It undercut the fundamental belief in America, the land of new life, liberty and pursuit of happiness for all. To deny this basic tenet of the American creed was unthinkable; therefore it was imperative to find the cause of the present anomalies and, by exposure, to correct them.

The conflict between a capitalist and his workmen appears frequently in the novels of the two decades.[27] It should be stressed, however, that in most cases, factories, technology, and the relations they present belong essentially to the American reality of the first half of the nineteenth century. The scale of their business operations is comparatively small, management still personal, and its relations with the workers, unless obviously abused, somewhat patriarchal. For most writers the struggle between employers and employees involves individuals rather than groups or social classes - the owner of a medium-sized mill or factory on the one hand and on the other, the local citizens who depend upon it for their living.[28] The world at large seems somewhat remote; the conflict has to be resolved just by the common sense and good will of people directly engaged in it.

Such an isolation from outside influences is often presented as helping to maintain proper relations between the employer and his hands. Both sides recognize their mutual dependence and need for one another. Under such conditions success is indeed within reach: personal merit, diligence, and intelligence are readily recognized and promoted. Richard, the handsome hero in T. B. Aldrich's novel The Stillwater Tragedy (1880) argues:

> Every soul of us has the privilege of
> bettering our condition if we have the
> brain and the industry to do it. Energy
> and intelligence come to the front . . .
> No door is shut against ability . . .
> whoever talks about privileged classes
> here does it to make mischief. There are
> certain small politicians who reap their
> harvest in times of public confusion.[29]

In fact, only a few discontented or restless men in
Stillwater fail to understand that there is no such
thing as a "square fight between labor and capital,"
some, less bright, can get intimidated or confused
for a time by false arguments, but most are reasonable
enough to realize that the dependence is mutual.
Stevens, a marblecutter, uses a well chosen metaphor
of Siamese twins:

> . . . if you were to pinch one of those
> fellows, the other would sing out. . . .
> When either of 'em fetched the other a
> clip, he knocked himself down. Labor
> and capital is jined just as those two
> was.[30]

As long as the terms of the deal are fair to both
parties and each keeps his side of the contract
honestly there is no reason for them to quarrel. The
workers, the novelists insist, are well able to
understand dull markets, falling prices, depressions
and other troubles affecting production and wages.
All it takes to win their support is to present the
difficulties to them and ask for their cooperation
as one would his equals. In Haworth's by Francis
Hodgson Burnett (1879), the hero who climbed to his
ownership of the steel mill from a poorhouse is able
to secure his hand's loyalty by appealing to their
sense of justice and fairplay.

> I'm not one o' the model soart . . .
> I've not set up soup kitchens nor
> given you flannel petticoats. I've
> looked sharp after you, and I should
> have been a fool if I hadn't. I
> let you alone out of work hours . . .
> Th' places I've built let no water in,
> and I let 'em to you as easy as I
> could and make no loss . . . I've
> given you your dues and stood by
> you . . . Then . . . them as Jem
> Haworth has stood by, let 'em stand by
> Jem Haworth![31]

John Hay indicates the same sense of equality as humans
and craftsmen of the same trade in the brief encounter
between Arthur Farnham and Sam Sleeny in The
Breadwinners (1884). One is rich and sophisticated,
the other, a slow-witted manual laborer, yet

> the two men talked a few minutes like
> old acquaintances; then . . . as he
> [Sleeny] turned to go both put out
> their hands at the same instant with
> an impulse that surprised each of them,
> and said "good morning."[32]

The recognition of their fellowship is spontaneous,
and if momentary, it is enough.

Conflicts are bred whenever overly proud, haughty
and vulgar men, however rich and college educated,
refuse to acknowledge this essential equality. M. A.
Foran in The Other Side (1886) indicates that the
struggle disrupting trade and disturbing public order
in Chicago results from the capitalists' failure to
treat workmen as fully human and to respect their
unalienable, democratic rights. To Alvan Relvason,
Richard's quiet but firm assertion that "the fact that
I'm the employed and you, the employer, does not in
itself make you superior or me inferior"[33] is more
than impudence. It is a sign of a dangerous, sub-
vertive spirit.

But then, Foran's novel is exceptional in several
ways. First of all, it takes place in Chicago, a
modern, urban conglomeration of diverse industries.
The struggle is no longer, at least not primarily, on
the personal level; it involves all producers co-
operating within the Board of Trade and the mass
of employees who are taking their first step toward
organization. Foran argues convincingly about their
right to form a union, to deal with the employers
through organization only. At the same time he
stresses their sense of order, respect for property
and ability to maintain self-control. Their demands,
though they seem outrageous to Relvason are reasonable
and just: they insist on full, weekly payment of
their wages and the right to trade wherever they
please.

Foran advocates two other remedies to end the
present industrial warfare: arbitration in labor
disputes (actually the first legislation concerning
arbitration was passed in 1886 in New York and
Massachusetts) and better education among workers.
His views are radical; admitting they are
revolutionary he hastens to explain he means "a
revolution in the realm of mind."[34] Not once does

27

he allow his characters to speak against the law or
ideals of the country - individualism, freedom, and
property. Foran's sympathy for the working class
cause was still rare in the 1880s. He wrote The Other
Side: A Social Study Based on Fact in 1886, his point
of view shaped by the recent events of the Haymarket
riots, where violence was actually provoked.

It is next to impossible to pin down the changes
in attitudes and sentiments concerning capital-labor
relations to any definite date. In real life, the
process was slow enough; its gradual drift into fiction
escapes any clear-cut classification. On the whole,
in the 1870s novelists may denounce the abuses and
injustice of new business methods but they tend to
describe and promote the model which is essentially
pre-Civil War and already well outdated. Their
attitude toward the labor movement is usually
negative, because they believed it undermined
American individualism, free competition and
democracy. The change occurs sometime during the
1880s, most probably pressed by the violence of
social struggle of the decade. The power of great
monopolies to control effectively all public
institutions on the one hand, and the increasing
destitution among the lower classes which was
threatening public safety and health on the other,
convinced a large section of society that control
and social legislation were indispensable. Thus,
the decade of the 1880s saw the first attempts to
check the total irresponsibility of the "robber
barons" - the enactment of the first State Arbitration
Law in New York and Massachusetts 1886, the Inter-
state Commerce Act 1887, culminating in the Sherman
Anti-trust Act of 1890. The muckraking journalism
and fiction of the next decade were very much a part
of the same process.

In the 1870s and 1880s, however, most novelists
regard the union movement either as a misguided
venture or as a conscious attempt to subvert American
individualism and self-help. If the road to success
stands open to quality, industry, and intelligence,
as they insist it does, there is no need to have
unions defending workers' interests. The able and
hard-working ask for no defense, others do not
deserve it. As often as not the novelists point out
that unions are actually run by the ignorant, shift-
less, and rough men who prefer easy popularity, free

28

drinks out of the union fund, and loafing to an
honest day's work. The most odious representation
of the labor movement is enclosed in John Hay's
The Breadwinners (1884). His dislike for the union
agitator Offitt is conveyed from his very first
appearance in the novel. Cast in the role of a
villain, he is "dark-skinned and unwholesome looking,"
lives in a squalid, ill-smelling tenement house on
a filthy alley, spends his time drinking, swearing,
scheming, but above all fanning discontent, grievances,
and the sense of injury with stereotyped slogans. He
argues about bloodsuckers and slaves, about a life or
death struggle against vampires "to get our rights
peaceably, if we can't get them any other way," but
when these fail to convince Sam Sleeny, he manipulates
his jealousy and anger at the man by whom he was
slighted. Hay makes a special point of Offitt's
determination to draw Sleeny into his Labor Reform.

> . . . [he] found a singular delight
> in tormenting the powerful young man.
> He felt a spontaneous hatred for
> him . . . his steady, contented
> industry excited in him a desire to
> pervert a workman whose daily life was
> a practical argument against the
> doctrines of socialism, by which Offitt
> made a part of his precarious living. . .[35]

Offitt is a thorough scoundrel with no decency or honor
in his heart; by the end of the novel he proves a
thief and a murderer. His worst crime, however, of
depraving and embittering two human souls cannot be
atoned or undone.

Abigail Roe distributes her objections to the
union movement among several characters of her Free,
Yet Forging Their Own Chains (1876). Hard-working
and sober Ned Malcome regards the union more as an
obstacle than a help in advancing his interests.

> . . . my objection to these unions is that
> they help support that class [the lazy
> and the inefficient] and prevent the
> really trustworthy men from earning an
> honest living.[36]

Also, both as a Christian and a citizen he will not
associate with people advocating violence whether

against people or property. Maurice Graham, the main
hero of the novel, upholds the principle of free,
individual choice against uniformity dictated
arbitrarily by the organization.

> But when compulsion is used, when a
> man's freedom of action is denied, and
> if he, rather than suffer want or run
> debt, is willing to work for less than
> his neighbors but cannot except with
> the risk to his life, then I call it
> mob-law, the worst kind of tyrany.[37]

Under normal conditions, i.e., a free and fair
contract, there is no good reason for the workers to
organize or strike. If they are occasionally driven
to such an extreme measure, it is primarily through
outside agitation or misinformation. A sudden cut
in wages is bound to kindle enmity. But it is the
owner's or manager's own fault if he lets ill
feelings brew without explaining honestly the true
reasons for the decision. Graham, the model
character, points out that the ten per cent cut
is actually an act of kindness, not exploitation.
What right have the owners to make their men do the
same work for ten per cent less?

> . . . just reverse the case and suppose
> you were the rich man . . . and the longer
> you continued working the less it paid
> . . . Your common sense and self-interest
> would tell you to stop . . . but we say
> to the men, that would be turning you
> out of work in mid-winter.[38]

Not trusting his hands to know the truth, the
capitalist lets them draw their own, mistaken
conclusions and put forth demands that cannot be met.
And if he is too proud to account for his decisions
to the workers, they take his refusal as confirming
their suspicion of being cheated out of their
rightful share of profit.

Much as with the question of success, the
novelists view the problem of unions and strikes
in a personal and individual perspective. The evil
lies not so much in greed, selfishness, or cruelty;
far more frequently it is rooted in the capitalist's
disregard for his hands as

> . . . men and women who have right to
> an interest in the fruit of their
> labor instead . . . like senseless
> machines whose work, either good or
> ill, was to be paid for like so much
> coal or water . . . no man has the
> right to degrade another man to the
> level of machinery.[39]

Human dignity is part of the argument. The other is
the workers' awareness that they depend on this one,
local factory for their living. Once the dispute or
strike is over, they will be coming back to operate
the very same machinery, for the benefit of the
owner and their own. They never wish "their" mill
removed to somewhere else; to destroy it would mean
to destroy their own lives. Thus, whatever violence
accompanies the strike it is not done by the honest,
well-meaning true-American workers. It is brought
from the outside by loafers, sneaky union demagogues,
ruffians and drunkards.

It is interesting to observe how closely the
popular fiction comes to the arguments advanced by
serious magazines whenever trade unions or strikes
are discussed. The novelists and journalists use
the very same ideas and almost identical vocabulary.
In his analysis of the labor question Edward L. Day,
for example, points out that trade unions foster more
antagonisms than they help to settle disputes; the
greater part of responsibility for the current
troubles falls to the unions since they press
arbitrary, irresponsible demands, oppose improvements, limit the number of apprentices, etc. Under
their tyranny, "the employer is now, perhaps, as
frequently the victim of oppression as are the
employed," while the individual workman "exchanged
the right of private contract, with all its dis-
abilities, for the despotism of the union which acts
as an effective bar to the industrial progress . . ."[40]
Such opinions could easily be pronounced by any of
John Hay's and Abigail Roe's fictional characters.
Washington Cladden, who as a journalist usually takes
a well-balanced, dispassionate view, admits that the
fears of social degradation among the working classes
are not groundless, hence their tendency to organize
and urge their interests is understandable. At the
same time he deplores the fact that both sides
involved in the conflict fail to see their common goal.

It is a sorry comment on our civilization that here, at the end of the
nineteenth Christian century, sane and
full grown men, whose welfare depends
wholly on the recognition of their mutual
interests and on the cooperation of their
efforts, would be ready to spend a good
share of their time in trying to cripple
or destroy one another.[41]

His bitter judgment could easily have been enclosed
in Foran's The Other Side.

The arguments propounded by the journalists
echo, and are echoed by, the novels of the time. This
affinity can be accounted for by the fact that, even
when they honestly try to be objective, the two groups
of writers represent, in the last analysis, the point
of view and interests of the upper middle class.
They could, and occasionally did, sympathise with
the hardships and privations of the lower ranks;
nevertheless social stratification, the law of
property and free competition were as sacred to them
as American democracy.

It would be too hasty a conclusion to infer from
the frequent appearance of strikes and labor disputes in various plots that the novelists were
particularly interested in the problem. To begin
with, few, if any, had a direct, first hand knowledge
of working class life and problems. The mill or
factory is present in the novel as a point of
reference, an important object in the local land-
scape, but the reader is seldom taken inside its
gates. Like his middle class narrator, he usually
remains outside observing the strange crowd of
preoccupied, angry, worried or exhausted people
hurrying to or from their work. His attention is
directed to external details - the deafening noise
of machinery, dirt and smoke, then physical weariness
stemming from the endless pressure of work. A rare
glimpse inside the workroom is designed to touch the
reader's sensibility.

. . . one hundred and fifty feet long,
and forty feet wide [the room] was next
to the roof and was lighted and ventilated
by small narrow windows at the front and
rear. The air was laden with fine dust

32

> and a sickening oily odor. There were
> four rows of machines extending the
> entire length of the hall. In this
> hot, ill-ventilated room or hall were
> crowded two hundred women and girls
> . . .[42]

But little is said about the actual work done, the
exertion, skills, and endurance it requires. Mary
Wilkins Freeman made a half-successful attempt to
render a personal response to work and the machine.
But Ellen Brewster, the heroine of The Portion of
Labor (1901) is young, strong, full of hope and
self-confidence; the revelation of the dignity of
labor and her exultation in participating in it is
perhaps probable, but without doubt uncommon.[43]

The best effort to record the experience of
the grinding factory system can be found in an
early short novel by Rebecca Harding Davis, Life
in the Iron Mills (1861). Unlike her contemporaries,
R. H. Davis avoids an emotional tone of the appeal
to pity. Her simple story is told with a direct-
ness and fidelity which indicate immediate and
personal observation.

> The mills for rolling iron are
> simply immense tent-like roofs,
> covering acres of ground, open
> on every side. Beneath these roofs
> Deborah looked in on a city of fires,
> that burned hot and fiercely in the
> night. Fire in every horrible form:
> pits of flame waving in the wind;
> liquid metal-flames writhing in
> tortuous streams through the sand;
> wide caldrons filled with boiling
> fire, over which bent ghastly wretches
> stirring the strange brewing and through
> all, crowds of half-clad men, looking
> like revengeful ghosts in the red light,
> hurried, throwing masses of glittering
> fire. It was like a street in Hell.[44]

Sordid details of life in the iron mills are neither
softened nor eliminated. Nor are they designed to
manipulate the reader's emotional response. Davis's
descriptions are remarkably exact. They convey a
sense of thwarted lives and wasted possibilities that

33

is still, and must have been then, profoundly disturbing. The startling korl sculpture serves as a symbolic image of the hero's life. The coarse, powerful female figure expresses his desperate hunger for things ever out of his reach - beauty, knowledge, understanding - of which he is but dimly aware. Thus, Rebecca H. Davis asks the fundamental question of human equality and justice.

On the whole, however, the novelist's interest is focused on the sentimental affairs of his middle class characters, not on dismal realities of the industrial era. The typical hero is an amiable young man who has to make his fortune in the world before he can ask his beloved to marry him. Whatever his initial social standing, he is presented engaged in some job in which success depends on his industry, integrity, skill, firmness, quick decisions and so on. Difficulties and temporary disappointments reveal his professional abilities as well as his moral character. If he is a manager, an engineer, a supervisor, poised between the owner and the hands, any conflict between the two can become a real test. To what extent does he identify with the interests of the owner? is he loyal and trustworthy enough to look after his employer's business at personal inconvenience or risk? is he man enough to face an angry crowd, to talk with the men, explain, remonstrate without yielding to pressures or threats? On the other hand, does he really care for the people he supervises? can he sympathise with their hardships, miseries and worries? is he ready to listen to their complaints, take their advice, consider their grievances and demands?

To offer his readers a plausible answer, the novelist sets his character in the midst of trouble for which he is not personally responsible but which he has to handle. (The reader is given to understand that the young man is wise enough to avoid mistakes made by the owner and were he free to act as he thinks right there would be no such conflict at all.) A strike serves the purpose best since it offers endless occasions to show the young man in action - reasoning with the workers, presenting his more advanced views and suggesting improvements to the owner (this always with due respect and self-respect), working hard and risking his life to save the factory from looting or destruction. A direct confrontation with the striking workers, in which he manages to

34

control and subdue their rebellious spirits by sheer
force of his personality balanced with clear,
rational arguments, seems a turning point in his
career as well as in the novel. The violence
latent in the crowd of frustrated and idle men can
create moments of suspense and excitement as
thrilling to the reader as Indians or Red-coats some
thirty years earlier. All the more so if the heroine
is caught in the midst of such a turmoil or, being
brave and loving, risks her life to carry an
important message or a warning. For example, in
Harold Frederic's novel The Lawton Girl (1890)
Jessica, although she is sick, ventures a desperate
two mile ride through a snowstorm to carry the news
of a planned attack on the Minster residence and back
again to bring Reuben Tracy just in time for him to
rescue the helpless women and their property. In
Miss Van Kortland by Frank Lee Benedict (1870),
Margaret Dane undertakes as risky a ride at night
to save the mine from looting, while the hero Prescott
courageously faces the mob. Abigail Roe takes her
characters through shooting, an attempt at murder,
and a flood before they can settle to live happily
ever after. There are countless variations on the
theme.

The novelists introduce strikes primarily to
enliven their plots; in spite of the apparent
surface realism of presentation they usually handle
their strikes as adventure, a source of danger,
unforseen turns of the plot, dramatic situations,
and tension. The capital-labor struggle becomes
in their hands a new formula of romantic adventure:
a modern American version of "cloak and dagger"
tales of the old continent.

The street-car strike episode in A Hazard of New
Fortunes (1890) echoes the actual events of 1886[45]
which disturbed the New York City transport soon
after Howells moved there from Boston. Transfering
his personal experience to Basil March, a respectable,
well-meaning, if ineffectual editor of a literary
magazine and something of the novelist's counterpart,
he concentrates on the New Yorkers' response to the
strike, as seen through press reports and gossip,
thus keeping it very much a minor incident in the
plot. The episode is brief, taking less than ten out
of four hundred and forty pages, and receives no

undue emphasis. Howells avoids the common mistake of
direct moralizing as well as refraining from turning
it into a melodramatic adventure. Carefully inter-
woven into the story, the brief scene of violence
becomes the turning point in the novel in the usual
Howells manner - almost by chance. There is no
connection between Christine's angry defiance at her
father's interference and the strike - except in time.
Dryfoos's fury is further provoked by lack of public
transport and by his son's decided, though unwillingly
spoken defense of the workers. But his violent blow
remains unrelated - except in time - to Conrad's
death. Howells leads his characters toward the climax
through a sequence of ordinary incidents and random
choices. Basil March goes first to the East and
then to the West side led by the curiosity "of a
philosophic observer." Conrad's sorrow and pity for
the workers' hopeless struggle converge with his love
when he responds to Margaret Vance's emotional
appeal for some unspecified peace action. His actual
presense at the particular place and moment of the
mob attack on a car, as much as March's, involves no
conscious decision. Lindau's presence on the spot is
not accounted for, yet it is fully consistent with his
behavior throughout the book. If his violent denounc-
iations draw the policeman's club to his person,
the shot that kills Conrad is fired at random. As
March scrambled out, "the fighting around the car in
the avenue ceased, the driver whipped his horses into
a gallop, and the place was left empty."[46] As far as
the characters are concerned, the strike is over at
this point; personal grief and troubles oust whatever
interest they may have had in the matter. Truly,
Conrad is killed in a riot, but it is his death, not
the street car strike, that alters the further
fortunes of the remaining characters.

In his handling of the strike Howells manages
to balance viewpoints and opinions to render justice
to the variety of human experience. Beaton's
egotism, Dryfoos' indomitable will to control and
overpower, March's intellectual distance, Fulkerson's
effervescent but shallow journalistic enthusiasm,
Conrad's Christian faith and compassion are fully
consistent with, and confirm, the reader's knowledge
and understanding of their psychological make-up.
Howells shifts from one character to another, careful
not to be limited by or to any single attitude, and
consequently not to impose any upon the reader. His

method of literary realism concurs with G. P. Lathrop's definition published in The Atlantic in 1874.

> Realism sets itself at work to consider
> characters and events which are
> apparently the most ordinary and
> uninteresting, in order to extract from
> these their full value and true meaning.
> It would apprehend in all particulars
> the connection between the familiar
> and the extraordinary, and the seen and
> the unseen of human nature. Beneath the
> deceptive cloak of outwardly uneventful
> days, it detects and endeavors to trace
> the outlines of the spirits that are
> hidden there; to measure the changes in
> their growth, to watch the symptoms of
> moral decay or regeneration, to fathom
> their histories of passionate or
> intellectual problems.[47]

For William Dean Howells realism was more than a consciously adopted writing technique. A shrewd observer, he skillfully chose such details of the contemporary scene whose commonplace familiarity would enhance the general plausibility of his story. Like all other elements introduced into the novel, his descriptions of poverty are never autonomous in the narrative. Discussed and meditated upon, these minor incidents add "roundness" to the characters. At the same time they offer Howells an opportunity to generalise and comment upon society at large.

In the early part of A Hazard of New Fortunes, the Marches come across a "decent-looking" man picking up whatever food can be found in the gutter and garbage heaps. The direct confrontation with hunger shocks and shames them both, yet all they can think of is to place a coin in his hand. The brief incident becomes a bitterly ironic comment on Isabel's complacent argument made only a few minutes earlier.

> I don't believe there's any real
> suffering - not real suffering - among
> those people; that is, it would be
> suffering from our point of view, but
> they've been used to it all their lives,

37

and they don't feel their discomfort
so much.[48]

The undeniable evidence to the contrary evokes a
purely emotional response: she refuses to live
in New York or any other place where such
destitution is possible, apparently oblivious to
or unaware that her ideal Boston has its own share
of poverty and suffering too. Her imperative,
idealistic demand "we must change the conditions"
as well as Basil's more pragmatic solution "Oh, no.
We must go to the theatre and forget them"[49] reflect
their helpless limitation: by disposition and habit
they are too engrossed in their own affairs. Also
they feel restricted by the established social
patterns, by their personal and family cares, by the
deeply ingrained need for physical and emotional
comfort. Their compassion for an individual in need
is genuine, but since they essentially endorse the
status quo, they find it easier to forget the
destitute than to engage in some unconventional action
on their behalf. It takes the extreme idealists
like Conrad Dryfoos and Margaret Vance to step out
of their comfortable existence in attempt to relieve
poverty in direct, personal contact.

Unwilling to be emotionally involved Basil March
seldom looks beyond the surface of the problem.
Metropolitan life holds many attractions for the
average reader who finds "those phases of low life,"
as March explains to Conrad, "immensely picturesque."[50]
He observes "the neglected opportunities of painters"[51]
in Chatham Square and Mott Street with an artist's or
sketchwriter's eye, trying not to see or think of the
hopeless struggle and misery of actual living there.

Admitting, as one probably should, that Howells
was correct in estimating the interest of the reading
public in picturesque poverty, one faces the dilemma
of evaluating the numerous articles on the subject
published in the magazines in the early 1870s. "The
Nether Side of New York" series by Edward Crapsey,
running in Galaxy March through September 1871, is
probably the most interesting example of factual
reporting. Scenes he describes and statistical
data he quotes could not but shock, all the more so
because throughout the text he keeps the dispassionate
tone of an objective though not uninvolved observer.
Other journalists tend to color their accounts,

appealing to the reader's sensibility or pushing the
picturesque and quaint local color to the front. Such
is the tone of Charles Dawson Shanley's writings for
The Atlantic 1869-1870.[52]

Regardless of motivation or dominant tone, these
articles provide ample information about the existing
poverty, especially about tenement housing and
homeless children. The steady inflow of immigrants
as well as of native country dwellers increased the
number of people crowded into tenements of New York,
Chicago and other industrial cities. In the post-
Civil War years poverty became the hardest social
problem which was rapidly becoming too extensive to
be dealt with by private charity. Significantly
enough, it was more often discussed in terms of
dangers it posed for the public than in terms of
individual human suffering. Public attention is
drawn to the fact that the over-crowded, ill-
ventilated, unsanitary tenements breed disease,
epidemics, and fevers which increase mortality rates
to seven, sometimes seventeen, per cent per annum.
The total lack of privacy, filth, crime, and bru-
tality to which all inhabitants, women and children
included, are constantly exposed, result inevitably
in social and moral degradation.

> The great metropolis, with its vast
> enterprise, its restless ingenuity,
> and its imperial revenues, can furnish
> its skilled labor, upon which its
> prosperity so largely depends, with
> no better than these . . . where they
> become negligent as citizens, and their
> children, owning to the influences which
> surround them, growing dangers to the
> commonwealth. . . . it is not strange
> that the civic virtues decay in a
> community where one half the people have
> no home . . . which is the foundation
> of public morality and intelligence.[53]

This disintegration of the family threatens to disrupt
the entire organization of society.

Similar passages can be found in the novels too.

> The crazy old building in which the
> Hacketts lived was a regular human

> hive. It had nothing suggestive of
> home. . . . It was a home for the
> Hacketts, for they had known no
> other. . . . In this building no
> family had less than two rooms, a
> fortunate contrast with those places
> not infrequent in the metropolis
> where a family of five or six persons
> cook, eat, live and sleep in a
> single room of moderate dimensions.[54]

And yet, there is a difference between the two kinds
of prose. The journalists present facts, occasionally
they point out the consequences of poverty, but they
rarely inquire into its causes. Dealing with the
same problem, the novelists seldom provide the reader
with detailed accounts; their descriptions tend to
be generalized and often reflect more the emotional
response of the spectator than they actually "paint"
the scene. Somehow they feel obliged to account for
the misery and want they present: the cause is
usually traced either to helpless ignorance or
personal wickedness.

The popular phrase "poor but honest" indicates
that a good many Americans of the time considered
poverty as linked with moral corruption and sin.
The novelists seem careful to distinguish between
simple, hard-working and frugal living which can
become an excellent school for young characters
and the harsher destitution which does not allow
even the basic decencies of family life. In An
Iron Crown (1885), Thomas Stuart Denison was not the
only one to emphasize the advantages of humble
origin, the very best stepping stone to success.

> It was greatly in young Wilson's
> favor that he had . . . to earn his
> own living. No school is so whole-
> some and efficient as the school of
> respectable poverty. The arduous
> labor and wholesome fare of farm
> life had developed a physical and
> mental structure, which was a splendid
> capital in itself to begin life on.[55]

In most novels of the later nineteenth century
sudden reversals of fortune form the staple element
of the plot. The middle class hero may find

him- or herself penniless overnight in consequence of
a bankruptcy or death. Such a temporary misfortune
becomes a crucial test of character - or manly
courage, responsibility and steady industry or, in
case of women, of endurance, patience, and loyalty.
The other stock situation presents poverty as
punishment, most often for the cardinal sin of
speculation. The novels abound in examples of
young men ruined both financially and morally by
speculation. Tom Norwell, the hero of An Iron Crown,
fails to learn the lesson from his father's bankruptcy (old Mr. Norwell was deceived by a friend);
too eager to win a fortune, he risks his and his
sister's scanty legacy and then her hard-earned
savings only to lose all in stock market gambling.
Blind to everything but money he trifles with love,
slights friendship and sisterly affection; by the
time he recognizes his fault and repents, gentle
and tender May, his fiancee, is dying of consumption.
The lovers are reconciled but then Tom leaves for the
West, alone and without a fortune, a sadder but
wiser man.

    The poverty-as-punishment theme had yet another
variant which could be applied to any character,
well or low born: penury resultant from weak will
enslaved by a wicked habit of drinking or drugs.[56]
The novelists dwell upon the culprit's moral degradation which may be slow but sure, yet the gradual
decline of his family seems a particularly rewarding
subject. Loss of a decent home, scarcity of
clothing, perennial lack of money for food and fuel,
and insecurity are endured by the patient wife and
bewildered children. While their hardships evoke
compassion, little if any excuse is offered for the
moral weakness of the offender. His timely death
may actually come as a relief to the suffering family
which then, through the efforts of a loving and
industrious son, may attain peace and modest comfort.
The more popular version leads the culprit through
moral reform and renunciation of evil, sometimes
expiation for wrongs, back to decency and human
fellowship.

    The novelist's perspective changes radically
as soon as poverty ceases to be a personal "trait" of
the hero and turns out to be a more general characteristic of a larger group. Then, he usually insists
that those who stay content with the modesty of

41

their actual condition suffer few wants because they
indulge in no extravagancies. And if they do, it
is through no fault of their own but because of
accident, death, illness or hard times. Following
this line of argument Amanda Douglas (Hope Mills,
1879) warrants that the greater part of suffering
among the working class is caused by waste and a
lack of the basic domestic skills: sewing, cooking,
baking, gardening, and the like. The ordinary wage-
earning family depends heavily on ready-made
industrial products which are usually of mediocre
quality. Whenever wages are reduced or prices go up,
they do not know how to provide for themselves in
the old way.

> Poor people - the real poor, I mean -
> are often wasteful and idle because they
> do not just know how to be any thing
> else.[57]

Their lives can be greatly improved by simple means
of education; once they are taught the necessary
skills they are able and eager to help themselves.

Until the very end of the century social justice
is usually interpreted in terms of individual honesty
and responsibility; there seems little awareness or
willingness to consider the problem in any wider
perspective. Without ignoring merciless exploitation
and frequent attrocities of the industrial system,
the novelists persistently present them as abuses
springing from greedy selfishness of the owner,
incidents marginal to the essentially noble and
beneficial process of manufacturing. As a free agent
the owner bears personal responsibility for the
quality of things done to his order, whether in
investments he makes or production he controls. No
excuse is offered for the selfish abuse of power his
money permits: all human misery caused by long hours,
disregard for health or safety, low wages, adultered
food provided by the factory store, and unsanitary,
overcrowded housing is traced to his door and most
emphatically condemned. Ignorance of how the other,
numerically much larger half lives[58] becomes yet
another proof of his indifference to the fate of
men whose daily toil provides his plenty and comfort.
Such a notion of failure both as a Christian and a
citizen dominates Elizabeth Stuart Phelps' novel
The Silent Partner (1871), one of few that actually

42

aims to present atrocities of modern industry.

Phelps' sharply focused picture includes Bob Mall who, because he is feeble with hunger, is caught by the machinery and killed, Cathy affected by noise and machine vibration in her pre-natal life and therefore born deaf and dumb,[59] girls who work too long to care for decency and slip into street walking still in their teens - to list just a few instances. The life of mill hands can hardly be called human: long hours (eleven and a half) and low wages reduce them to the level of beasts. The same vision of half-starved existence, warped by toil and care, fills the pages of Life in the Iron Mills by R. H. Davis, and also, though with not quite the same intensity, The Portion of Labor by Mary W. Freeman. Yet, opposing these novels, a more optimistic, cheerful view of lower class life seems to prevail in the nineteenth century fiction: for most writers the temptation to idealise proves too strong to be resisted. Two samples will illustrate the difference in tone and approach.

> Of late years all the fire of
> resistance had seemed to die out
> in the girl. She was unfailingly
> sweet, but nerveless . . . Often
> Maria felt vaguely as if she were
> in the grasp of some mighty machine
> worked by a mighty operator; she
> felt, as she pasted the linings, as
> if she herself were also a part of
> some monstruous scheme of work under
> greater hands than hers, and there was
> never any getting back of it. And
> always with it all there was that
> ceaseless, helpless, bewildered longing
> for something . . . Maria was half fed
> in every sense; she had not enough
> nourishing food for her body, nor love
> for her heart, nor exercise for her
> brain.[60]

Amanda Douglas' style rings a false note of too easy and cheerful optimism.

> Yet there was growing up among the
> hands a curious neighborly sympathy . . .

They were more intelligent; they kept
their houses cleaner, their gardens
prettier, not allowing them to go to
weeds before the summer was half over.
Those who could go to the industrial
school learned a deal about sewing,
and became seamstresses instead of
mill-girls. Some made their own
family dresses, some were very tasty
milliners. It gave them a reliance
upon what they could do themselves.[61]

If the novelists occasionally dwelt on the
unpleasant, ugly, and revolting scenes of contemporary
life, they did it with an aim other than just truth-
fully presenting reality. Some probably did find the
lower class life colorful, at least its less drastic
side, and used it for diversion, curiosity or
novelty. Most, however, tried to reach the
reader's emotions, to move him or her to pity,
perhaps - at least it was often the ostensible
purpose, to warn the unexperienced against the
devilish snares of the modern world. A preaching
tone can often be heard in the confidential asides
directly or indirectly addressed to the reader. And
yet there is comparatively little sensationalism in
the language or representation of social evils; the
tone of well-controlled, one is almost tempted to
say dignified, indignation outweighs sentimental
emotionalism. This self-imposed restraint, which
should not be identified with conventional propriety, effectively draws public attention to the
main goal of the novel - to measures and ways of
alleviating the lot of the nation's less fortunate
half. The suggestions proffered by the novelists
range from teaching Sunday School for the young
street vagrants (like Chetta Ingledoo in An Iron
Crown), or evening classes in home economics and
domestic industries (like Sylvie Barry in Hope Mills),
to setting up reading rooms for young people (Jessie
Lawton and Kate Munster in The Lawton Girl), coffee-
shops, clubs and co-operative stores (Jack Darcy in
Hope Mills). The fictional plots illustrate how such
ventures contribute to the general welfare and
order, first of all by keeping the young who are
vulnerable to insidious influences out of mischief,
secondly providing them with useful skills and
knowledge so that they can truly help themselves.
Last but not least, education makes the so far

ignorant and indifferent workers better i.e., self-reliant, intelligent and content citizens.

It seems significant that self-help and education gain unconditional approval while charity, in the ordinary sense of the word, is never offered as a final solution. Like many of their contemporaries, the novelists could have thought charity incompatible with the spirit of capitalism and self-reliance, or they must have tacitly shared the conviction that charity actually multiplies suffering and encourages irresponsible conduct and vice by offering relief and protection while it does nothing to prevent misery.[62] Barring gross misconduct and sudden exceptional misfortunes like death and illness, most hardships result from external conditions: inadequate housing, ignorance, exhaustion, malnutrition. Hence the evil can and should be removed by changing them, by building inexpensive but healthy homes, spreading education, providing wholesome entertainment, granting adequate pay for strenuous yet still humane work. It is both the duty and responsibility of the upper classes to provide "the other half" with these necessaries of life.

Many simpler educational measures which involve more time than money are within reach of open-minded generous ladies who can wake up interests, stir up latent energies and direct efforts. Their task is, perhaps, less spectacular, nevertheless important. The major improvement in the workers' lot as well as in turbulent capital-labor relations can be achieved through profit-sharing.[63] With a characteristic insistence numerous novelists argue the advantages of the system which involves neither condescending paternalism nor subversive socialistic doctrines. To dispel doubts or misgivings they have their characters discuss the matter thoroughly weighing all arguments for and against. Actually, all objections are easily dealt with. Some writers let their heroes actually test the theory in life, always with the very best results. Because the workers are personally interested in the outcome, they work better and waste less, while profits gained by joint effort are in fact no smaller for being shared with the hands. Thus, the fiction indicates that capital-labor warfare and dire poverty would disappear under the new system. No strikes, no conflicts, no undue

45

hardships; perfect trust and co-operation would replace hatred, selfishness and suspicion. The industrial millennium seemed within reach indeed.

In 1888 the kingdom of perfect equality, happiness, and order was proclaimed close at hand: present day confusion was but the first step toward a more sensible and just order. Edward Bellamy's utopia Looking Backward offered a simple yet radical solution to all problems upsetting American society. Rather than evoking the past models of business methods and social relations the way his many contemporaries did with nostalgia and regret, Bellamy dared to look ahead. If much of the present evil was caused by ruthless competition and pooling, the remedy should be sought in still more complete concentration of both capital and manufacturing which would eliminate rivalry. Bellamy transfers to political economy the old argument that the only remedy for the abuses of democracy lies in more democracy. In his utopia, business monopolies had been absorbed in one "Big Trust" - "of the people, by the people, and for the people," directed by the U.S. government. The state had become the sole investor, employer, and distributor. In the brief space of a hundred years humanity had reached a new level of civilization, becoming at last free from anxiety, want, injustice, crime and corruption, and able to enjoy high standards of ethics and culture as well as leisure and luxuries provided by technical development. Consistent with the most cherished American ideals, attainable through peaceful evolution of the present conditions, Bellamy's vision captured the imagination of his contemporaries. The book stayed a bestseller throughout the 1890s and, as James Hart concludes,

> left the nation an important legacy
> in creating a new picture of the good
> life, in dramatizing the benefits of
> mechanization, and in showing that a
> new deal for the individual rests on
> a collectivist program.[64]

The significance of Bellamy's novel lies, at least partly, in his basic affirmation of the current trend to combine and pool, a tendency which was denounced by some and lamented by others. Perfectly aware of the rapacity, exploitation and graft

46

thriving under the existing system, Bellamy realised
that the impulse to combine signified more than mere
elimination of unwanted competition to ensure larger
profits. It allowed far more efficient organization,
for the production of more goods which, if only
shared equally, could feed and clothe the needy.
Consciously or not, Bellamy shares the view of the
oil king, John Rockefeller who, as early as 1879,
claimed

> . . . this movement (toward monopoly)
> has revolutionized the way of doing
> business all over the world. The time
> was ripe for it. It had come, though
> all we saw at the moment was the need
> to save ourselves from wasteful
> conditions. . . . The day of combination
> is here to stay. Individualism is gone,
> never to return.[65]

The new scope of industrial and commercial
enterprise, the energy it harnessed with scrupulous
efficiency, commanded the respect of those whose
imagination was not fired by such spectacular
achievements. Pooling resources, capital, and
manpower allowed developments impossible under
the former mercantile conditions. The more
sanguine diagnosed the process as a clear manifestation of social Darwinism and welcomed the change
that opened limitless vistas of progress and general
welfare. Somewhat disenchanted realists recognised
the inevitability of both the bright and seedy
aspects of a monopoly system, acquiescing that
"syndicates are rotten but modern business can be
realised only by syndicates,"[66] while Jeffersonian
democrats seriously doubted if all the undisputable
advantages of material progress under new
arrangement balanced the evident abuses of corporate
business. The accumulated power of business magnates
to control, directly or indirectly, every sphere of
public life was threatening; their omnipresence and
omnipotence evoked dread mixed with awe. Individuals
as well as social groups felt helpless confronting
relentless dictates of railroad companies; trade and
smaller manufacturing branches had little choice but
to submit to prices and policies imposed by
corporations since they could hardly count on
defending their claims in fair trial and winning
unbiased verdicts at courts manipulated by the robber

barons at will. There must have been many who, like John Andross, the title character in Rebecca Harding Davis' novel (1874), thought monopoly no better, in fact no other, than the devil.

> As for its power - it [corporation] has money, unlimited money. It buys and sells at will the government and interests of the city where it belongs; it controls the press, the pulpit, the courts. The best men are muzzled by it, are forced against their will to serve it. . . . . You might fight against a man. But a powerful corporation meets you with the brain power of a multitude of men, but with no conscience, nothing to which you can appeal. It buys the law. It buys the public opinion.[67]

To general public the sudden rise of monopolies, within a brief span of ten or fifteen years (approximately between the late 1860s and early 1880s), which left no single branch of business unaffected, seemed a conclusive proof of some wicked conspiracy geared to subvert American democracy by destroying its moral and social order. To identify and expose the evil genius behind monopolies was regarded an imperative duty of every honest citizen.

The first and foremost objection to monopolies was their virtual control over smaller enterprises which they did not care to absorb. In order to eliminate competitors, Standard Oil for example offered them "a fair deal" of limiting production to a certain quota and fixing shipping arrangements with the appointed carrier.[68] The choice was to accept the terms or sell out, usually at a loss; the few who tried to fight for their independence were eventually squeezed out of the market. Such interference with personal freedom outraged many who believed it undercut the cardinal principle of American democracy. This argument, however prominent in actual struggles against monopolies, appeared but rarely in fiction.

In the final decades of the nineteenth century the overt condemnation of monopolies was continuously

48

cast into the individualistic mold. Most novelists
identified the complex corporate organization with
the men in charge of it, transfering their objections
against the system to a single person, somewhat god-
like in his power and imperviousness to outside
influences. He alone bears the blame for ruined
enterprises and individual bank depositors, for
arbitrary prices, for municipal graft, corrupt
legislatures, broken homes, estranged lovers, labor
riots. The choice could have been dictated by
necessity. Perhaps it was beyond these writers'
skills to convey the sense of a corporation as a
collective body: neither the novelistic techniques
nor language at their disposal provided adequate
tools for transcribing large scale operations of the
monopoly system. Keeping in mind, however, that the
prevailing experience saw the source of power of
corporations in their faultless organization, the
novelists' interpretation appears not so much
imposed by shortcomings in craftsmanship as motivated
by conscious choice. Whether the system is correct
or faulty, the responsibility for wrongs done
remains with men who operate within it.

The figure of a financial magnate was easily
incorporated into romantic adventures of a "boy meets
girl" plot; a villain could be rendered more odious
if he was as unscrupulous a schemer in his business
as in his sentimental affairs. Thus, a good many
novels of the 1870s feature a pitiless shark who,
whatever his designs concerning the heroine, brings
financial disaster to all who are entangled in his
machinations. His deals, however, are referred to in
general terms only; little is actually said of them
except that they are thoroughly dishonest. Somewhat
exceptionally, Joshua G. Holland (Sevenoaks, 1875)
recounts in detail Robert Belcher's scheme to fleece
villagers of their savings, the venture which brings
him one hundred and fifty thousand dollars. In these
early novels, the speculator-villain usually meets
the long-deserved punishment, overreaching himself
(Belcher in Sevenoaks) or being cheated in turn (Henry
Hunt in Free, Yet Forging Their Own Chains);
occasionally he escapes (like Horace Eastman in
Hope Mills), carrying off at least part of his booty.

Some novelists also introduce a minor figure of
a proficient schemer who acts as the tempter and the
evil genius of the business part of the novel. He

49

usually succeeds in profitting by his plots and manages to place himself beyond reach of legal or personal justice.[69] The pattern was duplicated frequently until the end of the century with but few variations. Charles Dudley Warner used it as late as 1889 in A Little Journey in the World. Characteristically for this later period, Rodney Henderson, the main male character of the novel is an unscrupulous yet extremely successfuly stock market dealer. Warner focuses his attention on the worldly progress of Margaret, Henderson's wife; nevertheless, this assigning the leading role to a dubious character seems a new departure toward an avowed admiration for financial tycoons and novels of business adventure like Drieser's Cowperwood trilogy.

Popular fiction makes a curious but marked distinction between industry and finance. Somehow the novelists seem convinced that manufacturing is fundamentally legitimate and sound. The owner may be accused of exploitation and hard-hearted self-ishness, nevertheless his business methods are honest enough. What distinguishes the villains of the business world in popular novels is that they have graduated from industry to the dubious realm of the stock exchange. Though the necessity of financial operations for a modern economy is fully recognised, a profound lack of confidence in them persisted for a long time. The novelists argue that stocks and bonds should offer small as well as large investors steady and secure income at moderate rates of interest; constant buying and selling is symptomatic of a restless spirit or gambling fever, both tempting man to speculate.

In popular fiction of the time speculation is anathama. Unstable stock exchanges unscrupulously manipulated by bulls and bears render regular operations impossible. A sudden panic may paralyse the market, freeze credit, undermine general trust in investments, and discourage capital in general. At the same time spectacular gains made by the few lucky ones - gains earned, as Howells put it, without effort or merit - beguile the unexperienced to try their luck, as often as not only to become an easy prey of crafty manipulators. In this gambling fever nothing remains sacred - neither love, nor duty, nor honor, nor friendship. Pages of fiction are filled with victims robbed of their all by those whom they

50

trust. The number of those who having yielded to
temptation are betrayed and ruined morally as well
as financially is equally large.

Like other forms of gambling, speculation is
akin to addiction, yet doubly insidious, for even
the one whose will is not enslaved by the evil fever
finds it next to impossible to extricate himself from
the many entanglements - to keep his gains he has
to go on playing.[70] Illicitly accumulated wealth
spreads its unwholesome influence to all areas of
public life, but the novelists devote most attention
to graft on the one hand and the extravagance of
fashionable society on the other. No doubt both
subjects offered varied possibilities for romantic
and sentimental adventure.

The novelists regularly complain that the
art of making money is learned quicker than the
art of using it. A foolish desire to keep up with
the millionaires strained many a family budget
beyond the breaking point and pushed the husband
to rash, dubious or risky deals to gain what the
wife had already spent. In The Cliff-Dwellers (1893)
by Henry Fuller, Jessie Ogden is by no means the
only fictional "girl in very moderate circumstances
who spent all her time in going about among wealthy
relatives and friends."[71] When married, she fails
to realize her husband is a young man on a moderate
salary and cannot possibly match the unlimited wealth
of the Atwaters and the Inglases. The characters
become totally absorbed in feverish acquisition,
which is stamped with "that devil-on-two-sticks, the
dollar mark."[72] No time, energy or desire is left
for things of the mind or heart: marriages become
estranged (Aria and Clayton White in Queen Money),
family life disintegrates (the Ingledees in An Iron
Crown or the Brainards in The Cliff-Dwellers),
literary and artistic interests are forgotten
(Margaret in A Little Journey in the World)--all
human values are reduced to, if not replaced by,
money.

If frivolous extravagance had pernicious effects
on society, it seemed a minor transgression when
compared with the political corruption for which the
1870s were infamous. It was bad enough to have
railroads, built at public expense, and industries,
exploiting the natural resources of the nation, both

51

refusing to recognize any duty or obligation to the
people. But to see government, legislatures and
courts turned into obedient tools and promoting
the interests of monopolies awoke bitterness and
resentment. The generation of robber barons
insisted on their absolute right to use "private
property" as they pleased without interference.[73]
It was only toward the end of the century, in the
1890s, when price competition was replaced by
competition in efficiency, that the notion of public
service entered business policies. The early period
was dominated by the attitude "public be damned."
The reform movement demanding more respect for law
did effect change; to assess its share with any
precision, however, is virtually impossible.

The novels of the period dealt with political
corruption frequently drawing material from numerous
scandals of the 1870s - the Erie Railroad affair
(1868), Black Friday (1869), the Tweed Ring (1871),
Crédit Mobilier (1873), the Whisky Ring (1875), the
details of which were published extensively in newspapers and magazines.[74] The first to transfer them
into fiction was Mark Twain, whose The Gilded Age,
written in collaboration with Charles Dudley Warner,
gave its name to the era. Twain and Warner include
almost all the disreputable practices of the decade;
incidents, characters, and deals are easily traceable
to actual persons and doings.[75]

Other novels followed Twain's success: John W.
DeForest's Honest John Vane, published in 1875 after
being serialized in The Atlantic (July - November
1873), Rebecca Harding Davis' John Andross in 1874,
and Francis Hodgson Burnett's Through One Administration in 1882 (first serialized in The Century,
November 1881 through April 1882). The four novels
as well as two short stories by John DeForest -
"An Inspired Lobbyist" (The Atlantic, December 1872)
and "The Other Fellow" (The Atlantic, December 1878)
deal with corrupt legislatures. They reveal ways
and means by which basically honest people abuse
power and public trust. Many men, elected like
John Vane or Andross to represent the public
interest, prove unequal to the task - scanty education
lends feeble support to common sense while their
uprightness, not grounded in conscious moral training,
remains superficial. Their probity lasts as long
as it is not tested; lacking firmness they yield to

pressures and temptations, often only half realising
the extent of their fall.

> . . . he [John Vane] had never been
> beneficient and unselfish. He had
> no moral sympathy enough to feel the
> beauty of virtue in the individual,
> nor intellect enough to discover the
> necessity of virtue to the prosperity
> of society, nor culture enough . . .
> Considering the bare poverty of his
> spiritual part . . . it was no wonder
> that, once temptation got him faced
> hellwards, he rode to the devil with
> astonishing rapidity.[76]

The problem becomes truly vicious when moral weakness
is linked with ambition. Both John Vane and John
Andross are pressured by their worldly wives who
desire social prominence at any price. Since
Andross is too honest to be bribed, the skillful
lobbyist manipulates him through his pretty and
selfish wife. Shaped by circumstances and his
associates rather than by moral conscience, Richard
Amory (Through One Administration) falls as much
through his ambition to have a career as through
the desire for profit.

These early novels offer readers one side of
the problem. They expose the mechanics of corruption -
accumulated money exerting overpowering pressure on
ordinary people who are often placed in a dis-
advantage. Without excusing the guilty, the novelists
seem to indicate that the responsibility rests, at
least partly, with the voters. Those most capable
of fulfilling public duty shirk politics, thus leaving
the rule of the country to the ignorant and the
unscrupulous.

> The rich and intelligent kept on . . .
> building fine houses, and bringing up
> children to hate politics as they
> did. . . . There was hardly a
> millionaire on Alonquin Avenue who knew
> where the ward meetings of his party
> were held. There was not an Irish
> laborer in the city but knew his way
> to his ward club as well as to mass.[77]

In the 1880s the perspective seems to have shifted
from the corrupted to the very source of evil - the
almighty financier. His schemes to multiply wealth
brook no interference, but to complete them he needs
favorable legislation. T. S. Denison comments on
some newer procedures which ensure docile legislatures
and courts:

> It is a comparative innovation for
> railroads to make judges of the
> higher courts. Their making of
> United States senators has ceased to
> attract attention, if it ever did.
> As to making Congressmen and members
> of State Legislatures that is not
> worth the trouble. They can be
> bought ready-made much cheaper.[78]

Writing on poverty or the labor movement, the
novelists suggested more or less workable improvements.
But faced with the bribery and corruption destroying
the very core of the political system, they seem
strangely helpless. They bring evil to light,
they enumerate consequences, they name the guilty
but offer no remedies to curb abuses. In this
context an early article (Galaxy, November 1869)
signed by "an American Positivist" warrants special
attention. The author recognizes the power that
aggregated money gives to corporations and individuals,
as well as the pure selfishness of the influence it
exerts. The question is how to control it.

> Now wealth and enormous social and
> political power it wields by its very
> existence, is one of those facts which
> cannot be ignored. We must accept
> it . . . To destroy wealth or take
> away the power it naturally gives to
> its possessor, is impossible. . . .
> Accept the inevitable. Capital has
> power. Make it personal, responsible.
> Put the capitalist in authority instead
> of his creatures, the lawyers and
> politicians . . . Hold him responsible.
> The next greatest power in modern
> civilization after wealth is public
> opinion. . . . When this spiritual
> power has its proper recognized organs . . .
> it will be able to control wealth.[79]

The author is perhaps the first to see the free press
as an instrument capable of informing and shaping
public opinion. By exposing the truth, revealing
secret deals and underlying motives or goals of
interested parties, it can forewarn and forearm the
public against encroachments on its freedom and
democratic rights. Two novelists, Henry Keenan
and Will Payne, dramatize such action, both dwelling
at length on the dangers and difficulties involved in
collecting desired information (who bribes whom for
what and how much is usually a well guarded secret).
Even partial victories are worth winning.

> Of course, it was not unprecedented.
> Other cases of that kind had been
> presented to the public. Probably
> when it came to the State's attorney's
> office everybody in the net would
> wriggle out . . . But Leggett . . .
> knew that he could convict Dexter in
> public opinion.[80]

Leggett's immediate, somewhat selfish aim is to
strengthen the financial position of the Eagle and
attain its secure control as its editor. In the
world ruled by money, to keep a newspaper independent
is no small achievement. At the beginning of his
journalistic career Fred Carow (The Money Makers,
1885) is informed of the futility of any campaign
against the money kings.

> The men who are running this country
> just now are not groping in the dark. . .
> What you have seen of their methods ought
> to have taught you that they are not men
> to be balked by one newspaper, or a dozen.
> When a newspaper opposes them they find
> means of buying it out.[81]

Not daunted by this prospect Carew leads the struggle,
wins a political victory for his party and establishes
his full control, financial and editorial, over the
independent Eagle. (The prospering city of Valado
where the action takes place closely resembles Chicago
as described by Payne in The Money Captain. Is not
the independent Eagle in the two novels the same
newspaper?)

Novels set in Washington usually mix stock situations signifying local flavor with an innovation in the character of a brilliant female lobbyist. Apparently, during the seventies "the women lobbyist was seen everywhere, making streets and hotels disreputably gay."[82] To induce a Congressman or senator to promote a bill by any available means was disreputable enough; each proposition was supposed to be judged and voted upon its own merits. But a beautiful and intelligent woman using her feminine attractiveness to play upon masculine vulnerability, in order to beguile a man to act against his own better judgment, was revolting. It is a clear sign of depravity. Laura Hawkin's success (The Gilded Age) brings disgrace to true and pure womanhood. For this very reason, Bertha Amory (Through One Administration), those ambitious husband imposes the role upon her, is almost tragic.

> In all events, Richard has talked to
> me a great deal. It is plainly my
> duty to be agreeable and hospitable
> to the people he wishes to please and
> bring in contact with each other. . . .
> I am that glittering being, the female
> lobbyist. I wonder if they all begin
> as innocently as I did and find the
> descent . . . as easy and natural.
> . . . When we get our bill through . . .
> I am to go abroad for a year . . . that is
> the bribe which has been offered me. One
> must always be bribed, you know.[83]

A close look at the late nineteenth century novels, especially the popular kind, indicates two motives behind their writing. They were obviously written for entertainment. The sentimental adventures of their young heroes met the reading public's demand for action and suspense, while offering momentary escape from commonplace daily affairs into the realm of excitement, emotions, and wish-fulfillment. From this point of view those novels are something like modern fairy tales. Their literary and artistic merits are few and far between, so their interest today is solely that of a "period piece." The romance plots usually follow such simple formulas that the first fifteen or twenty pages give the clue to the happy ending two or three hundred pages later.

The wish to educate, however, seems as prominent
in popular novels as that to amuse; actually the two
complement and balance one another. Set in contemporary, familiar scenes, they provided vidid,
imaginative illustration of evils and dangers
screened by deceptive fair appearances. Thus, all
simple-minded and simple-hearted readers could be
put on guard against perils amidst which they lived,
oblivious of their existence. Those in precarious
financial or social positions could profit by an
early warning of possible disorders, by suggestions
of remedies and self-help, and - by no means
unimportant - they were given hope for a happy
ending somewhat similar to that of fictional heroes.
Last but not least, the popular novel offered
vicarious experience of perils and victories with
all their attendant excitements, to be enjoyed at
a safe, comfortable distance.

Exposing social evils of the time - poverty,
exploitation, corruption - the novelists appeal to
the reader's pity and sense of justice, assuming
that, moved by his conscience, he would strive to
relieve misery and atone abuses. They may be
appalled or puzzled by the social chaos prevailing
in American life. They may be disturbed by the
rapid disappearance of familiar sights and customs
or feel nostalgic for the golden days of innocent,
agrarian America. Whether they lament or denounce,
they nevertheless all share a fundamental belief
in man's natural goodness and open possibilities
of progress. This belief lies at the core of Mark
Twain's A Connecticut Yankee in King Arthur's Court.
Neither the author nor the hero doubt the benefits
of the industrial age; their enthusiasm for practical
efficiency, modern comforts, and above all empirical
common sense equals their ardent allegiance to human
equality and democratic government. Everett Carter
argues that the tragic ending of the novel was
dictated by historical necessity.

> . . . progress and democracy had not,
> after all, come to the Western world
> in the sixth century. And there are
> undoubtedly some of the stirrings of
> uneasiness with the validity of the
> American idea, an uneasiness that
> would deepen into pessimism and
> then to nihilistic despair of his

> late years . . . This was not yet the
> feeling projected by A Connecticut
> Yankee.[84]

The final scene with twenty five thousand men killed
in an instant by the electric current seems to
question the ultimate value of machinery and
efficient organization. While recognizing his
defeat in victory, Hank's faith in the blessings of
the industrial order is not shaken. Nor is Mark
Twain's at this point, unless one reads into the
novel a criticism never intended by the author.

The world described by Mark Twain and his
contemporaries is ruled by a universal moral law,
therefore evil is never an abstract force in it.
Wickedness and corruption, however widespread and
dominant in social organization, are always traced
down to individuals. No external circumstances or
pressures diminish personal responsibility for
whatever wrongs are done, be they small or large.
The hero's actions motivated by selfishness, greed,
or ambition cannot be excused; if he falls to
temptation, his very weakness of character renders
him contemptible. Although some novelists allow
the hero to hesitate a bit when making moral
choices or momentarily slip from rightousness, they
tend to divide their characters into sheep and goats,
admitting little traffic from one side to the other.
The wicked meet their well deserved punishment in
the shape of bankruptcy, violent death or defeat in
courtship, while the just enjoy all the blessings of
a fair fortune and a fair heroine. At the end of the
novel they settle down to live ever after as a happy
family.

According to the long standing narrative
tradition, to the victor belongs the spoil; at the
same time his failure to secure the prize, i.e.
fortune and love, signals unmistakably the narrator's
condemnation of his behavior. In the 1870s and 1880s,
this convention was seldom questioned, though some
writers like Twin and James avoided the issue.
William Dean Howells was perhaps too much a part of
the establishment to defy it openly like Theodore
Dreiser did in Sister Carrie (1900). Nevertheless
in 1896 he seemed reluctant to follow its pattern.

Dealing with the success theme in The Landlord
at Lion's Head (1896), Howells distributes his clues

so carefully as to leave judgment to the reader alone. Jeff Durgin, a rough and ill-mannered country boy, grows to be a Harvard student and apparently something of a gentleman. Yet his rise from obscurity to affluence is neither due to nor accompanied by any spiritual refinement. His selfishness and his fierce, vindictive temperament prove no obstacle to success: so far as his experience goes the doctrine of reward and retribution is but an old-fashioned superstition.

> Prosperity or adversity, they've nothing
> to do with conduct. If you're a strong
> man, you get there, and if you're a weak
> man, all the righteousness in the universe
> won't help you. . . . I shall be blessed
> if I look out for myself; and if I
> don't, I shall suffer for my want of
> foresight. But I shan't suffer for
> anything else.[85]

Jeff denies the basic rule of the success code with impunity. Truly, he fails to win the heroine, nevertheless he marries, and happily a girl of a considerably higher social rank than his own. Then, unexpected events including his mother's death and the burning of an old building help him realize his ambition: he becomes the sole owner and manager of a prospering, fashionable summer hotel. There can be no doubt about his success.

Throughout the story, Westover, who is the central consciousness of the novel, heartily dislikes Jeff's ideas and behavior, but Howells tones down his disapproval by making him an oversensitive and somewhat effeminate character. Though he expresses many of the author's own opinions, his point of view should not be regarded as final. Howells balances his negative attitude with the more optimistic view voiced by Whitwell, a true Yankee.

> Well, all that I thought . . . is't
> there must be a moral government of
> the universe somewheres, and if a bad
> feller is to get along and prosper
> hand over hand, that way, don't it
> look kind of as if - . . . What's
> the use of thinkin' a man can't
> change? Wan't there ever anything
> in that old idee of a change of heart?

Perhaps Whitwell is more generous in his rustic
simplicity than Westover, but his leniency may just
as well reflect his corrupted imagination and his
conscience confounded by the prosperity of the
unjust.[86]

With all the genuine involvement in current
social problems, the novels of the 1870s and 1880s
fall behind their time: the exemplary business they
advocated was already an anachronism under the
spreading monopoly system, and the success ideal they
promoted proved unattainable for most who aspired to
achieve it. Popular conviction insisted that, though
the road to social advancement was long and difficult,
opportunities remained ever open, only perhaps less
numerous. Alfred Thimm documents how easily such an
illusion could be created and maintained.

> . . . there exists overwhelming
> evidence of an amazing social
> mobility which can only be
> underemphasized if it is compared
> to the claims of the Horatio Alger
> myth. By the standards of any
> society, past or present, the
> constant renewal of an upper class
> by thirty to forty per cent is very
> impressive. Only if the actual
> mobility is measured against the
> exaggerated claims of the business
> ideology does it become worthwhile
> to emphasize that the majority of
> American businessmen came from a
> highly select group which most
> certainly did not consist of poor
> farmers, workers and immigrants. . .[87]

Discussing the same phenomenon a recent textbook on
American history explains that the mistaken notion of
unrestricted mobility was hardly avoidable under the
circumstances.

> This was hardly avoidable, given the
> overwhelming proportion of poor
> families in the nineteenth century
> society and the rapid growth in white
> collar jobs for which candidates had
> to be found. But very few poor boys
> were likely to reach the pinacle of
> the white collar employment. Jobs at

the top were reserved, by and large,
for the sons of middle- and upper-
class businessmen and professionals,
old family in origin, Episcopal or
Presbyterian in religion, urban in
upbringing, and college educated.[88]

A sense of probability kept most novelists from making
mistakes on this point. Excepting Horatio Alger,
they set their heroes against middle class backgrounds. The "bottom" from which they climb upwards
means in fact the lower bracket of the middle class.
Arriving at the top, they remain, in fiction much
as they did in fact, faithful to the values of their
native environment.

Taking a somewhat one-sided view of the contemporary situation the novelists seem unaware that
a large section of business community looked with
little favor upon price competition, which impaired
the stability of the market. From the very beginning,
the steady drive toward pooling, agreements, and
combinations was bitterly opposed by farmers and
small, local business owners. But a good many
accepted this new form of cooperation, even if it
meant a degree of subservience, because it promised
a smaller but steady and secure margin of profit.
In the world of finance and business any solution
was preferable to chaos and waste.

The prevalent economic uncertainty
also challenged the business community
to bring disorder under control, to
substitute order and calculation
for confusion, to "rationalize" . . .
the conduct of business.[89]

A degree of blindness in the matter is not really
surprising. If some businessmen accommodated to
technical and organizational innovations with relief,
others did the same from necessity - new business
methods offered a definite workable solution at least
to some problems. This pragmatic approach, however,
did not affect their professed beliefs concerning
the ways of doing business, free competition, and
success. Whatever policies they were actually
following, they tended to see themselves as winners
in the struggle for success and, as a rule, upheld
tenaciously the old creed of rugged individualism,
occasionally flavored with new catch phrase "the

61

survival of the fittest." This fact could have been reason enough for the novelists to continue promoting old views and ideals, either disregarding actual practices or denouncing their sordid details as moral corruption.

Rooted in Benjamin Franklin's <u>Autobiography</u> on one hand and Jefferson's vision of <u>agrarian America</u> on the other, the success ideology was, as both Rex Burns and Richard Weise use the term, a yeoman dream of another era.[90] In the final decades of the nineteenth century the world of local enterprises, individualistic ventures, and independent craftsmen existed no more, except in a wish dream. Therefore the ideology it produced was no longer relevant.

> The new American soil was not fertile
> ground for the yeoman individualism of
> an earlier day. . . . The myth of success
> and the literature it produced in the
> nineteenth century was an expression of
> the pre-industrial mind in America. Its
> decline was prefigured by the disappear-
> ance of its social frame of reference.[91]

Under such unfavorable conditions the novelists of the time made a serious attempt to adopt the model of success to new circumstances. In part they accommodated change, shifting their heroes from manufacturing and trade to engineering, management, and finance. Furthermore, they consistently redefined success in terms of human values rather than money and material gains. The key to success remains, as before, in character. The hero has to prove himself first of all as a Christian - firm in moral virtues, kind and compassionate as well as honest and just. Secondly, to succeed means to become a responsible, useful citizen. If wealth and education place him in the upper ranks of society, his public duty involves

> . . . the investment of effort or
> time or money, carefully considered
> with the relation to the power of
> employing people at renumerative
> wage, to expand and develop resources
> at hand and to give opportunity for
> progress and healthful labor where
> it did not exist before.[92]

Wealth is his gain, but not his alone, therefore it should benefit society and not be wasted on selfish whims and dissipation. A character in a humbler position fulfills his duty by offering diligent, honest work for his pay and providing a stable, happy home for his family. Finally, no one becomes truly a success unless he becomes something of a gentleman. The process involves the education of body and mind, acquiring polite manners, self-control, and dignity, together with generosity and refinement of the soul.

Thus, the novelists of the time sided with the reform movement in exposing and condemning the unrestrained drive for acquisition. The price society pays for this lack of self-control is heavy, though many fail to recognize the cost. Materialism replaces idealism, selfishness kills patriotism, while social life, devoid of grace and culture, centers on the vulgar display of dollar worth.

> We have made poverty more disreputable than dishonesty. . . . Our avarice of prosperity, our passion of advancement become more and more unscrupulous, and less and less admit the interference of conscience and taste.[93]

Such criticism, voiced by writers of self-help pamphlets, journalists as well as the novelists, is usually balanced in fiction with prospects of a nobler and finer life in which quality takes precedence over quantity and cultural refinement is treasured above millions. Thus, the popular novel recognizes success only when the hero's excellent character leads him to fulfill his duty as a citizen; his aspiration to higher aims complements his business concerns. In doing so, the novelists seem to project a desirable state of affairs rather than reflect the actual one. And yet, their picture remains true.

> The insistence of the novel that everyone who obeys the norm grows rich and happy is, of course, not consistent with what can be observed in ordinary life; it is true to norms but not to life.[94]

In the confusion of the changing industrial reality
of the last quarter of the nineteenth century, the
novelists consistently uphold the old norms and
make them the principal framework and point of
reference for the fictional worlds they create.

Notes

1. Cf. Irving G. Wyllis, The Self-Made Man (New York, 1954). The author analyses dozens of handbooks of self-help to build the meaning of the term success in all its varieties. The main value of the book is that the concept is considered in a comprehensive social context, in relation to education, family, environment, religion, and business. Yet, he presents it as a component of social mythology, the functioning and permanence of which are based on common belief, an act of faith beyond proofs of the rational mind.

2. James D. Mill, The Art of Money Making (New York, 1872), p. iv.

3. L. U. Reavis, Thoughts for Young Men of America (New York, 1873), p. 25.

4. Cf. O. S. Marden, The Young Man Entering Business (New York, 1903), pp. 7-9; and N. C. Fowler, The Boy, How to Help Him Succeed (Boston, 1902), pp. 67-69.

5. E. F. Clark, Danger Signals (Boston, 1885), p. 141; cf. Mill, p. 65.

6. Cf. Andrew Carnegie, Empire of Business (New York, 1902), p. 224; Fowler, p. 73.

7. Those born in the 1830s seem particularly privileged: James Fiske - born 1834, Andrew Carnegie - 1835, Jay Gould - 1836, Pierpont Morgan - 1837, John Wenemaker - 1838, John Rockefeller - 1839, Leland Stanford, somewhat older - 1825.

8. E. P. Briggs, Fifty Years on the Road (Philadelphia, 1911), H. C. Brockmeyer, A Mechanic's Diary (Washington, D.C., 1910), Carnegie, Autobiography (Boston, 1920).

9. Lee Lowenthal, Literature, Popular Culture, and Society (Englewood Cliffs, N.J., 1961), p. 113.

10. J. G. Cawelti, Apostles of Self-Made Men (Chicago, 1965), p. 120.

11. James D. Hart, The Popular Book (Berkeley, 1961), p. 161.

12. Mark Twain, "The Story of the Good Little Boy Who Did Not Prosper," Galaxy, May 1870, pp. 724-28.

13. Henry W. Sedley, "Our Ranch at Zion," Galaxy, September 1876, p. 376.

14. M. E. W. Sherwood, "The Outside of the Cup," Galaxy, March 1874, p. 484. "He [Alfred] was beyond, above the necessity of work, but his natural cleverness brought him a ready and easy superiority . . . [he] went on, becoming a more and more accomplished failure. Every kind of success awaited him but successful success, he failed professionally for want of persistency. He failed in business for want of meanness . . . Finally he lost his character."

15. Henry James, "A Passionate Pilgrim," The Atlantic, April 1871, p. 496.

16. Cf. E. E. Hale, "How Fr. Frye Would Have Preached It," The Atlantic, February 1867, p. 282. "It is so much easier to earn an extra than to economize. . . it is the haste to be rich which is dangerous. But it is not the detection and punishment which play the dog with a man. It is meanness and lying, after the first excitement of the enterprise is over."

17. W. D. Howells, The Rise of Silas Lapham (New York, 1965), pp. 5, 19.

18. Howells, A Hazard of New Fortunes (New York, 1965), p. 226.

19. Ibid., p. 193.

20. Howells, Silas Lapham, p. 43.

21. Ibid., p. 250.

22. Ibid., p. 320.

23. Noting down the "impressions of a New England summer," Sarah Orne Jewett records a poor farmer using the cliche phrases and characteristic

success rhetoric, "I've done the best I could . . .
but everything seems to have been ag'in us; we
never seem to get forehand. . . . But my oldest
boy, he's getting ahead some, he pushed off this
spring and he works in a box-shop in Boston; . . .
I don't see how he done it, but he's smart,
if he only keeps his chance." "Deephaven
Excursions," The Atlantic, September 1876, p. 282.

24. Joan Rockwell, Fact in Fiction (London, 1974),
    p. 4.

25. Howard Mumfred Jones compiled a partial list of
    important innovations in The Age of Energy (New
    York, 1973), p. 157.

26. Hart, p. 107.

27. This part of the discussion on business relations,
    trade unions, and strikes is based on ten novels:
    F. L. Benedict, Miss Van Kortland (1870), Abigail
    Roe, Free, Yet Forging Their Own Chains (1876),
    F. H. Burnett, Howarth's (1879), A. M. Douglas,
    Hope Mills (1879), T. B. Aldrich, The Stillwater
    Tragedy (1880), John Hay, The Breadwinners (1884),
    M. A. Foran, The Other Side (1886), W. D.
    Howells, A Hazard of New Fortunes (1890),
    Harold Frederic, The Lawton Girl (1890), M. E. W.
    Freeman, The Portion of Labor (1901). For the
    best treatment of the strike in American fiction
    see F. M. Blake, The Strike in the American Novel,
    (Metuchen, N.J., 1972).

28. "In the birth era of such leviathans as Standard
    Oil and US Steel, many a writer continued to lay
    the scene of his economic problem novel in a mid
    century New England mill town, and to treat the
    capital-labor conflict as if it were solely
    a struggle between individual employer and local
    employee." W. F. Taylor, The Economic Novel in
    America (New York, 1973), p. 68.

29. T. B. Aldrich, The Stillwater Tragedy (Boston,
    1880), p. 144.

30. Ibid., p. 196. The same metaphor is used by Maud
    Howe in "A Strike," The Century, October 1888,
    p. 819: "Your mill is the capital but what good
    is the mill without the men? It was like trying
    to divorce the Siamese twins of capital and

labor. It meant death to both."

31. F. H. Burnett, Howarth's (New York, 1879), p. 188.

32. John Hay, The Breadwinners (New York, 1884), p. 96.

33. M. A. Foran, The Other Side (Washington, D.C., 1886), p. 76.

34. Ibid., p. 437.

35. Hay, p. 86.

36. Abigail Roe, Free, Yet Forging Their Own Chains (New York, 1876), p. 57.

37. Ibid., pp. 33-34.

38. Ibid., p. 33.

39. Maud Howe, p. 819.

40. E. L. Day, "The Labor Question," The Century, July 1886, pp. 400-401.

41. Washington Gladden, "Is it Peace or War?", The Century, August 1886, p. 572.

42. Foran, p. 98.

43. ". . . she [Ellen] was fairly exultant. All at once she entered a vast room in which eager men were already at the machines with frantic zeal. . . . When she felt the vibration of the floor under her feet, when she saw people spring to their stations of toil . . . it seemed to her that the greatest thing in the whole world was work. . . . She realized all at once and forever the dignity of labor. . . . She never again felt that she was too good for her labor, for labor had revealed itself to her like a goddess behind a sordid veil," M. E. W. Freeman, The Portion of Labor (New York, 1901), p. 350.

44. R. H. Davis, Life in the Iron Mills (Old Westbury, N.Y., 1972), p. 20.

45. "In 1886, in the very year in which he moved to New York and just prior to the enactment of the State Arbitration Law, the city experienced

a serious traction strike, which lasted for months and was accompanied by violence: no car was driven without a police guard. This strike and difficulties of voluntary arbitrarion both figure in A Hazard of New Fortunes - two out of a number of instances in which Howells not only disclosed a knowledge of the contemporary scene, but drew his material directly from it." Taylor, p. 236.

46. Howells, A Hazard of New Fortunes, p. 369.

47. G. P. Lathrop, "The Novel and Its Future," The Atlantic, September 1874, p. 321.

48. Howells, A Hazard of New Fortunes, p. 60.

49. Ibid., p. 61.

50. Ibid., p. 129.

51. Ibid., p. 160.

52. The following samples will illustrate the difference: "Generally ragged, often hatless or shoeless, or both, unclean in person and language, the newsboys are a class by themselves. . . . Out at four o'clock in the morning to crowd the foldingrooms of the morning newspapers, they can be seen from then until late at night, when they are vending the evening journals, scouring every part of the city and heard everywhere shouting their wares into the general ear. Each sale they make yields only a cent or a fraction of a cent profit, and it can be readily seen that they must make many sales, involving hours of time and a terrible strain upon youthful muscles, for them to gain even a scanty subsistence. If a boy sells one hundred papers per day, he is doing more than an average business, but his profits amount only to about fifty cents: so that three dollars per week is more than the general reward of an occupation that consumes fourteen hours per day and requires a daily capital almost equal to the weekly profits." Edward Crapsey, "The Nether Side of New York, Outcast Children," Galaxy, September 1871, p. 360. And the other: "Sometimes, on Sunday, the bigger ones may be seen polishing each other's shoes, and this service is performed absolutely on the reciprocal principle,

and free of charge. Observe yonder two boys, one
of them with him whole-cloth Sunday trousers on,
the other veneered as to his legs with partial
pantaloons, the original material of which is past
detection amid the patches innumerable with
which it has been supplemented. The first boy,
as he kneels down to clean a customer's boots,
places a folded newspaper between his knees and
the ground. The other would probably take no
such precaution, even had he trousers worth
saving. One cannot help thinking that there may
be a possible millionaire in number one, while
number two may never have a pair of knees, perhaps, between which and the dirt the inter-
position of an old newspaper would be worth
while." Charles Dawson Shanley, "The Small Arabs
of New York," The Atlantic, March 1869, p. 283.

53. Crapsey, "The Nether Side of New York, Tenement
Life," Galaxy, August 1871, pp. 175-76.

54. T. S. Denison, An Iron Crown (Chicago, 1885), p.
129.

55. Ibid., p. 28.

56. Cf. H. P. Roe, Without a Home (New York, 1881)
for opium addiction, and his Barrier Burned
Away (New York, 1885), for an intemperence
subplot. Also see Yates, a minor figure in J. G.
Holland, Sevenoaks (New York, 1875).

57. Amanda Douglas, Hope Mills (Boston, 1879), p. 139.

58. The phrase was commonly used. Foran elaborates
the metphor so that no reader can miss its
meaning: "One half the people on this earth are
ignorant of how the other half live, nor do they
care to know. There is so much bliss in ignorance
that they resent any attempt to put to one side
the gilded screen that conceals the dark side of
life." The Other Side, p. 99. Also see Howells,
A Hazard of New Fortunes, p. 126. In 1890 Jacob
Riis published his shocking photographic study of
slum conditions titled How the Other Half Lives.

59. Cf. Foran's combination of journalistic and
moralizing prose: "Out on one of these streets,
reeking with noxious exhalations and miasmatic
poison, crouching and cowering in the foot or two

70

of shade next to the hot walls of the buildings,
were long lines of ragged children, whose pinched
faces were . . . old and worn, though young in
years. . . . It is the ill-fed, over-worked, and
half-clothed mother that gives birth to the
child whose face is 'a ghostly caricature of age.'
The accumulated wrongs, hardships and privations
of the ancestor leave their hideous and damning
impress upon posterity; and ante-natal conditions
could be mainly attributed the causes that
made the faces of these children a mockery of
childhood." The Other Side, p. 88.

60. M. W. Freeman, The Portion of Labor, p. 309.

61. A. M. Douglas, Hope Mills, p. 348.

62. Cf. D. McMaans, "The Suppression of Pauperism,"
The Century, March 1884.

63. Cf. Douglas, Foran and A. Roe.

64. Hart estimates that while only 10,000 copies were
sold during the first year, by December 1899 "it
was selling weekly as many copies as had been
sold in its entire first 12 months, "reaching
nearly a million copies during the 1890s." The
Popular Book, p. 171.

65. Quoted after Hofstadter, Miller and Aaron, The
American Republic, vol. 2 (Englewood Cliffs, N.J.,
1967), p. 47.

66. Morals in Modern Business (Yale, 1909), p. 43.

67. R. H. Davis, John Andross (New York, 1874), pp.
52-53.

68. Ida Tarbel, History of the Standard Oil Company
(New York, 1904).

69. For examples see Stokes in Free, Yet Forging Their
Own Chains, Wandover in The Lawton Girl, and
Carver in Queen Money.

70. "Temptation [to speculate] is only at the
beginning. After a man gets far enough along
in a thing he belongs to it; he has to go on,
. . . With everybody scrambling and clutching,
even if you're lucky enough to grab something,

you must take the chance of somebody else grabbing
it away while you're reaching for another piece."
Will Payne, The Money Captain (Chicago, 1898),
p. 159.

71. H. S. Fuller, The Cliff-Dwellers (New York, 1893),
     p. 273.

72. G. A. Hibbard, "The Woman in the Case," The
     Century, June 1889, p. 210.

73. "The company had their capital of sixty millions
     and nearly twelve million acres of land
     free. . . . What did Uncle Sam get in return?
     The privilege of paying for a railroad without
     the right of owning or controlling it." Denison,
     p. 77. "If they [the people] build a road and
     give it to me, then it's my private property.
     I'll do as I please with it. I'll charge what I
     please for freights. If they don't like it let
     them grumble as they please." Ibid., p. 313.

74. Of numerous articles on current public affairs
     special attention should be given to James Parton's
     series: "Log-rolling at Washington," "The Small
     Sins of Congress," and "Uncle Sam's Treatment
     of His Servants" (The Atlantic, September,
     November, December 1869 respectively). Also on
     the railroads: "The Great Erie Imbroglio" (The
     Atlantic, July 1868). J. S. Black, "A Great
     Lawsuit and a Field Fight," (Galaxy, March 1872),
     J. A. Coleman, "The Fight of a Man With A
     Railroad" (The Atlantic, December 1872), W. M.
     Grosvenor, "The Railroads and the Farms," (The
     Atlantic, November 1873), C. F. Adams series,
     (The Atlantic, January through June 1876).

75. "Of characters, Laura Hawkins was certainly
     suggested by Mrs. Laura Fair of California, who had
     recently been acquitted of murder on the ground
     of emotional insanity. Senator Dilworthy was
     drawn from Senator Pomeroy of Kansas, and the
     activities of Willis M. Weed and his associates
     so closely resemble these of the Tweed Ring of
     New York that the picture is practically
     undisguised. Among the dupes of the speculative
     game, Washington Hawkins was suggested by Orion
     Clemens: and the effervescent Colonel Sellers, in
     all probability, a relative of Mark Twain's,
     James Lampton," Taylor, pp. 124-25.

76. J. W. DeForest, Honest John Vane, The Atlantic,
    October 1873, p. 446. Cf. Denison, p. 58.
    "Heretofore he had succeeded in preserving his
    honor. . . . He felt that he was completely in
    the power of these two men, even though he was
    a rising and highly successful lawyer. There
    was no denying that he was largely indebted to
    Ophir for his success. To hold back now would
    seem base ingratitude, - furthermore it would
    be ruin. Somebody else would do the work and
    reap the reward if he refused. The things
    demanded were wrong and dishonorable, but they
    were an evil of the times not of his making.
    If a great free people were willing to have their
    rights trampled under foot, they did not deserve
    to be free. Besides, he conscientiously believed
    the party they were fighting was much worse
    than his own. He would do the work. If it
    soiled his hands a little, he would profit by it
    sufficiently to be able to buy gloves for the
    rest of his life."

77. Hay, p. 247. Cf. Denison, p. 302: "The better
    classes have no right to complain of misgovern-
    ment and corruption, so long as they refuse to
    perform their duties at the primaries and at
    the polls."

78. Denison, p. 56.

79. An American Positivist, "What To Do With Wealth?,"
    Galaxy, November 1869, p. 707.

80. Payne, p. 172.

81. Henry Keenan, The Money Makers (New York, 1885),
    p. 39.

82. Taylor, p. 125.

83. Burnett, Through One Administration (New York,
    1901), p. 424.

84. Everett Carter, The American Optimism (Chapel
    Hill, N.C., 1977), pp. 225-26.

85. Howells, The Landlord at Lion's Head (New York,
    1964), p. 234.

86. Ibid., pp. 301, 303.

87. Alfred Thimm, Business Ideologies in the Reform-Progressive Era, 1860-1914 (University, Al. 1976), p. 95.

88. Hofstedter et al, p. 2043.

89. E. C. Kirkland, Dream and Thought in the Business Community, 1860-1900 (Ithaca, N.Y., 1956), p. 26.

90. Rex Burns, Success in America (Amherst, Mass., 1976); Richard Weiss, The American Myth of Success (New York, 1969).

91. Weiss, p. 118.

92. Rockefeller, Random Reminiscences of Man and Events, quoted after Kirkland, p. 154.

93. Eugene Benson, "To-Day," Galaxy, November 1867, p. 816.

94. Rockwell, p. 104.

Part Two

WOMEN

Ideal womanhood

The dramatic experience of the Civil War brought Americans a fresh awareness of differences and discrepancies between the regions. To the generation surviving the war a discovery of a deeper unity above and beyond apparent diversity was vitally important to endow their bitter struggle with meaning. Hence, after 1865, American society awaited a new expression of its identity which would blend variety into a unified national experience.

On the economic level, post-war industrial development leveled great many local differences, creating conditions and problems basically the same all over the country. Consolidated mass production enforced standardization in manufacturing. At the same time technical inventions helped to spread a comparable uniformity in other areas of life. The telegraph and telephone gave the smallest and remotest communities full access to information and news service; the transcontinental railroad system supplied all local markets with the very same goods, while the circulation of magazines shaped tastes and needs all over the country according to a single pattern.

The search for a comprehensive national culture accounts for the prevalence of eclecticism in taste, art, ideas, and forms of expression. Eclecticism allowed a free mixture of diverse, discordant elements and could accommodate variety with ease, although the artistic effect of such a miscellany was more often striking than aesthetically satisfying. In the final decades of the nineteenth century, American culture was not tainted by bohemian freedom from constraint: pursued and cultivated primarily at home or in comparatively small society circles, it was closely associated with family life.[1] Hence, characteristically for the age, it was marked by propriety and middle class responsibility.

The tendency toward unity can be best observed on the level of ideology. Whatever its other functions, the concept of success helped to fuse regional and

75

environmental differences, imposing a uniform standard
of model behavior, principles, and goals for the
entire male population of the United States. It was
complemented by a parallel model of exemplary woman.

An average American male felt, perhaps, equal to
the demands of the success code; however, to live up to
the ideal womanhood he was supposed to worship and
marry must have been a difficult task indeed. He was
measured by his work and achievements. Her most
valuable accomplishments were rooted in her very
nature; education and training merely brought them to
the surface. In other words, he was judged by what
he did, she by what she was: thus, the differences
between them were as marked as between two species.
In his short story "The White Cowl" (1888), James Lane
Allen draws a portrait which could well bewilder a more
sophisticated hereo than his innocent and simple monk.

> Do you know who are most like you monks
> in consecration of life? It is the woman.
> . . . They work for others as you have
> never worked, they pray for others as you
> have never prayed. In sickness and
> weariness, day and night, they deny them-
> selves and sacrifice themselves. . . .
> They keep themselves pure and make others
> pure. . . . if you wish to find vigils
> and patience and charity - go to the good
> women of the world. They are . . . in
> home, and school, and hospitals, with
> the old, the suffering, the dying.
> Sometimes they are clinging to the
> thankless, the dissolute, the cruel;
> sometimes they are ministering to the
> weary, the heart-broken, the deserted.[2]

Woman is a saint. Her actions, as listed by Allen,
reveal the essentially feminine qualities of goodness,
tender kindness, and faithful concern for others, while
patience, meekness, and endurance offset the unequal
physical strength of the guardian angel. Woman's
personal beauty and charm are more than physical
attributes; they are read as signs of spiritual grace
and virtue. If only protected from material want and
anxiety for her loved ones, woman's spirit soars above
ordinary sordid cares seeking beauty and refinement.
Made of finer substance, she is more sensitive to the
ennobling influence of art, especially of music. Her

delicate sensibility and intuition, which add subtlety
and clarity to her perception of moral issues involved
in human actions, destine her to be the "keeper of the
keys to the Kingdom," a judge as well as a guide to
all entrusted to her care.

To love her is a privilege, an inspiration which
guards man against temptations of the wicked world
and his own baser inclinations. Popular novels and
tales relish in depicting how ardent but reverent
love guides the hero to righteousness. "The Woman in
the Case" by George A. Hibbard is as good an example
as any.

> I loved her as a strong man, not yet
> wholly lost, loves the marvel of the
> earth, a good woman; loved her as a
> man . . . not unfamiliar with evil,
> can love the woman who represents to
> him all that there is of good, . . .
> for him who so loves there is a rule,
> ever present, ever strong to control
> evil, to restrain passion, quick to
> mold and direct character, acts,
> career.[3]

Hibbard closes his short story with an ironic twist.
Inspired and uplifted by his love, Alston becomes
morally upright and financially prosperous, but the
woman in the case - idealized and worshipped for years-
was, in fact, neither good nor noble. Having ruined
her husband she ran away with another man and finally
died in misery, sickness and shame.

The power to direct man's moral choices and conduct involves a corresponding responsibility for
turning feminine gifts and graces to their proper
purpose. There are few graver sins than using them to
wake up love or passion only to scorn it.

> She [Ada Hunt] knows that she had used
> his [God's] gift of beauty as a lure to
> gratify her vanity or selfish designs,
> . . . she had sent men from her presence,
> robbed of all faith in what was pure and
> true and of good report.[4]

A woman thus misusing her calling incapacitated herself
for love and therefore for happiness; at the same time

her mischief poisoned the principal spring urging man
to nobler, disinterested actions. Deprived of the
ideal and powerful incentive he was more likely to
yield to the selfish, greedy, and corrupt influence of
the modern, i.e. industrial order. Furthermore, such
an experience bred disrespect, if not outright contempt, for women in general, attitudes hampering a true
advancement of civilization.[5]

In popular fiction of the second half of the
nineteenth century most female characters, except a
few wicked ones, share spiritual excellence, as
reflected in their beauty and alluring charms. Minor
figures are occasionally drawn to indicate physical
frailty: they have slender forms that the slightest
brow might ruin forever, wasted and pallid cheeks with
spots of color too brilliant for health, and thin,
white and tremulous hands which signal imminent sickness and death. By contrast the heroine's fresh,
smooth skin and clear sparkling eyes signify her
active, vigorous temperament, full of keen interest
in life and confident self-command. The true American
girl, as seen and portrayed by Howard Chandler Christy,

> has successfully appropriated to herself
> the best qualities from all the different
> races to which she owes her origins . . .
> is not of a city or a state, but the
> whole boundless continent is here.[6]

The novelists availed themselves of the type frequently
to present model behavior suitable for any young lady.
Since they addressed predominantly middle class
audiences, their heroines and their ideological bias
bear the same bourgois character.

Little Women (1868) by Louisa May Alcott, a best
seller in 1868-1869, illustrates the proper, in fact
the only way to attain the ideal. Marmee, the
exemplary mother of the family, is too wise and loves
her daughters too well to indulge their natural
inclinations to selfishness, vanity, laziness, or
frivolity. Step by step, the four girls learn that
true beauty and worth begin with self-control, faithful attendance to everyday duties and tender concern
for needs and comforts of others. They grow to
appreciate the moderate comforts of their busy, happy
home above the shallow brilliance of luxurious idleness, to value generosity and magnanimity more than

calculated shrewdness, financial gain, and self-
interest. Whatever their girlish dreams, desires, or
rebellions, they sooner or later realize their true
calling to love and be loved. By the end of the novel
they all find personal fulfillment and happiness as
wives, mothers and homemakers.

Of the four March girls, tomboy Jo was perhaps
the most attractive because she introduced the element
of adventure, daring, color, and the unexpected. Her
further fortunes, narrated some years later in Little
Men (1871), appear somewhat unconventional, but only
on the surface. Too lively and impulsive to become
another Marmee like her older sister Meg, Jo nevertheless adheres to the very same values and norms
against which she once rebelled and works as patiently
as her mother to instill them in her young wards -
though using different methods. The two novels are
obviously designed to invite young readers to identify
with the fictional characters and emulate them. And
if we are to trust another novelist, Jean Webster and
her Aga Abbot's remark "I believe I'm the only girl in
college who was not brought up on Little Women,"[7] they
functioned this way for nearly forty years.

Like many of her contemporaries, Louisa Alcott
views her characters - young as they are at the
beginning of the novel - in terms of their future
roles. Since they are girls, they are expected to
marry, bear and bring up children. Their greatest
happiness and reward is to see the husband enjoy
their society more than the pleasures of a newspaper
or a cigar. In the fictional world, all interests
yield to the supreme goal of making a comfortable
home for him. A novelist may admit some additional
occupation but, significantly, it never interferes with
the heroine's domestic duties.

Model characters, like Sylvie Barry in Amanda
Douglas' Hope Mills (1879), embody all the desirable
virtues and exemplify the right course of action.
Descendent of "old American stock," Sylvia is brought
up in modest comfort, leisurely enough to allow some
artistic and intellectual pursuits, but withdrawn
from fashionable circles and encouraging economy and
domestic skills. Pretty, good, wise, self-controlled,
she and her likes are more often to be found in the
country or in small provincial towns than in the
bustling metropolis, which are frequently presented

as nests of all evil.

This, however, was not the rule. Lucy Florian in _Queen Money_ by Ellen O. Kirk (1889) is Sylvia's counterpart among New York society. She belongs to the same old New York aristocracy remembered fondly and described by Edith Wharton. By birth, then, Lucy has every right and opportunity to move in the very best circles but "she had a true Vanderwater contempt for being fashionable though fashionable people amused her."[8] Faithful to the values of mind and character, she prefers to remain an outside observer, detached from the prevailing hustle to become rich or socially prominent.

Respectable young ladies like Sylvia and Lucy follow no career because there is little for them to learn or gain: they are perfect. As often as not, they act as the moral conscience of the novel, setting standards for other characters, especially men. By word or more simply by expectant trust, they release dormant spiritual energies in men, thus stirring them to act honorably and generously, to resist temptations, to aim high and accomplish noble deeds. Their uplifting influence is ever gentle and tender, exquisitely feminine in its indirect subtlety and grace, but nevertheless powerful and irresistible.[9] In the course of the novel they fall in love with suitable young men of sterling character and promising future, thus achieving happiness and maturity. As wives and mothers they will instill the same virtues in the younger generation. Unfortunely, model characters are usually flat. In course of the novel they neither learn anything nor grow up or develop; instead they remain essentially static. At best they serve as an educational foil for the sins and follies of others; with less skillful writers they become mere mouthpieces of the author.

Obviously enough, not all "American Girls" met the absolute standard even in fiction, not to mention reality. Counteracting the popular image Howells and James offered their more critical, perhaps more realistic versions of the type. If their portraits are so much better, it is due to literary talent and depth of vision which enabled them to convey social and psychological complexity. Their two heroines Lydia Blood (Howells, _The Lady of the Aroostook_, 1879) and Daisy Miller (James, _Daisy Miller_, 1879) are very different individuals. The two are placed in somewhat

similar, socially ambiguous situations of going around
unchaperoned, yet Lydia is "saved" and marries at the
end of the novel while Daisy is "lost" and eventually
dies of Roman fever.

A heir to New England tradition, Lydia is aware of
the possibility of sin and corruption latent in human
nature, therefore she gives her full and conscious
consent to be governed by moral principles, and
secondarily by social conventions. Her natural self-
possession is of a feminine, passive kind, trained in
obedience and self-discipline. Throughout the voyage
of the Aroostook she remains unaware of the impropriety
of her being the only woman aboard. Once in Venice,
she quickly comes to understand the situation and,
though ashamed of her new knowledge and revolted by
the "moral degeneration" of Europe, she is willing
to comply with the custom of the country in this respect.

Lacking such native tradition and home training,
Daisy is even less prepared to deal with the problem.
Her character, totally unused to restriction, is guided
solely by her own caprice and fancy. Her independence
is close to being wild, disciplined by neither moral
nor conventional precepts. Her mother is not fit
to counsel her, but then, Daisy is not likely to
accept anybody's judgment or advice except her own.
Her ignorance equals her innocence. Furthermore she
refuses to be taught, helped, or protected, forgetting,
or perhaps never growing to realize, that people are
usually judged by the appearances, not by purity of
heart. Finally her boldness and disregard for
convention become ambiguous even to the best in-
tentioned. Persistent in following her own mind she
is eventually defeated.

It seems Henry James considered such lack of self-
control a particularly characteristic feature of
American society.[10] The uniform respect and protection
accorded to American women encourage confident and
unreserved manners even in chance encounters. The sense
of security leads them to behave in public with the
same serenity and ease as in the intimate family
circle. Granted every privilege and honor due to
royalty, they accept the status without self-doubt or
hesitation, usually without a sense of any obligation
involved. Men's unconditional, uncritical approval
blinds women to the very possibility of a more pleasing
and satisfying social behavior. Never confronted with

81

demands and requirements, they can hardly develop any
notion of superiority to which they could aspire.
Thus, they stay serenely content with their own bold,
noisy conduct, vulgar in its superficial brilliance.
From James' point of view, spontaneity has some,
though limited, grace; setting no direct opposition
between the two concepts he emphasizes that culture
is produced through a long and conscious training
imposing discipline and restraint on the minutest
aspects of human behavior. The question remains
whether James would find fault with the exemplary
Sylvia Barry or Lucy Florian – or would they force
him to admit exceptions to his sweeping criticism?

Aside from very unequal artistic merits, the
difference between E. O. Kirk, Abigail Roe, and
L. M. Alcott on the one hand and Howells and James
on the other procedes from the writers' intended
purposes and goals. The question of the writers'
respective sex seems irrelevant. The three women
novelists present or rather recommend an ideal;
Howells and James remain content with depicting
ordinary mortals who, nevertheless, are measured by
the very same ideal. This implicit judgment of the
audience is skillfully incorporated into both <u>Daisy
Miller</u> and <u>The</u> <u>Lady</u> <u>of</u> <u>the</u> <u>Aroostook</u>. Thus, the
question arises whether the ideal was true or false.
If a girl was induced to believe herself better,
nobler, or purer by the mere fact of her womanhood,
she was perhaps likely to practice these virtues;
instilling them in her children she perpetuated the
relevance of the idealized image. Thus, fiction
could influence reality. On the other hand, she was
as frequently warned against too confident reliance
on the excellent qualities ascribed to her by the
ideal. Without denying its validity, serious
journalists and authors of numerous guides and advice
books felt an urgent need to balance it with down-to-
earth matters. They repeatedly emphasized the necessity
of a thorough training in the traditional domestic
skills which gave a girl considerable advantages on
the matrimonial exchange of the society, and after-
wards.

> To a prudent man who lives by his work,
> the knowledge that the girl can make a
> dress and cook a beefsteak, however
> prosaic it may sound to sentimental
> ear, is a gratifying information.[11]

Love and courtship may be romantic, but commonplace
duties of housekeeping which follow the wedding are
not. Wealth and leisure reduce heavy tasks, but the
ordeal of keeping, training, and controlling servants
usually proves as absorbing and tiresome. Various
projects to reform household affairs through
phalansteries or cooperative movements which aim at
relieving the hardest and most irksome duties are but
half measures. The best organized services cannot
eliminate all work involved in managing a home and
family life.

Numerous books and pamphlets instructed young
girls on a variety of subjects. Cooking and sewing
were considered of primary importance: much attention
was given to personal cleanliness, healthy diet,
sensible dressing and sanitation, with special emphasis
on the value of fresh air, cold water, and exercising.
Etiquette books, for example, argued that health and
hygiene were prerequisites to beauty and should be
practiced for their own sake, yet courtesy and regard
for others demanded the same.[12] Pamphlets advocating
dress reform and spreading advanced views on medical
care and prevention were probably as numerous as those
peddling quack tonics and patent medicine, therefore
their respective impact upon the general public remains
impossible to assess. This vast literature of
counselling and advice sponsored all the objectives
of various reform programs, purity and temperance
crusades being not the least among them. But a great
many books concerning the everyday affairs of an
average middle class household seem to be directed at
balancing and correcting false notions of love,
marriage and family duties as derived from sentimental
fiction.

> Fiction has given us a host of improbable
> wives in improbable white dresses, living
> in improbable cottages, and serving
> improbable deserts of strawberries and
> cream to certain equally improbable hus-
> bands. Do not . . . fashion your ideas
> after any such pattern. Real life is
> a different thing.[13]

Such guidebooks generally offered young women simple,
sound and practical advice. To follow it required
no special qualifications of mind except common
sense; nor did it involve any extra expense. On the
contrary, the purpose is to show young, unexperienced

wives how to make the most of their moderate means.

The idealizing reverence was supposed to balance,
some say to compensate, the manifest inferiority of
women in other areas: the physical and mental capacities
which barred them from full participation in external
affairs. Active public life was considered incompatible with woman's true calling of homemaking and
motherhood. The above notion could not become
ingrained in mass consciousness until the frontier
experience was separated from actuality by a
generation's lifetime. As long as the frontier stayed
open and the recent memory of its enterprising and
rough life-style disavowed all charges of infirmity
and helplessness, the etheral ideal of feminine
frailty could not captivate the popular imagination.
Helen Papashvily's ironic comment argues the point
with her usual sharpness.

> At twenty five, perhaps, she had crossed
> a wilderness, raised a cabin, brained a
> panther, outwitted an Indian, improvised
> a corn shelter, set a broken leg, brought
> in a crop, and traded a setting of eggs
> into a dairy herd. At fifty such a woman
> must have laughed in her fan . . . when
> gentlemen solemnly declared the female
> constitution would collapse under the
> strain of voting, managing money, or
> studying for a profession.[14]

The frontier was no place for lily-flower women. Yet
the two "variants" of ideal women existed side by side
for a long time. Changes wrought by the Industrial
Revolution opened the way to a more general acceptance
of the feminine ideal, nevertheless it hardly applied
to the working classes, and only partially to the
lower middle class. In the 1870s a society girl from
eastern urban centers seldom had an opportunity to meet
the self-reliant, active woman described by Papashvily,
because they rarely moved in the same circles.

The wife-and-mother perspective which dominates
nineteenth century fiction was seriously questioned by
many thinkers and journalists. Their arguments, discussed below, revolve around the elementary truth best
phrased by Julie Caroline Dorr.

> There is a vast deal of nonsense written
> and spoken on matters pertaining to woman,

> her work and her destiny. . . . it is
> woman's glorious destiny to be a wife
> and mother. Is it? Then it is man's
> to be husband and father. But is there
> any reason why he should be nothing
> else?[15]

With clarity of perception and common sense J. C. Dorr
opposes the prevailing but too narrow perspective
limiting men and women, but especially women, to
aspects defined by sex. Such a ramification, important
as it is for social organization, should be secondary
to the commonly shared lot and experience as human
beings. The contemporary novelists, however, seem
reluctant to share Dorr's arguments: if they did, they
kept their convictions out of their fiction. Most
writers, particularly those addressing the mass public
reproduce the ideal of "true womanhood" - an angel, a
mother, and a goddess all in one. And yet, one observes
a surprising number of contradictory opinions concerning
this lofty creature. She is sublime but often silly;
she can endure hardships, face and defy dangers, but
her frailty demands constant support and protection;
she will discern subtle moral issues yet the simple
accounting for expenditure exceeds her mental capacity.
Furthermore, she is worshipped as much as she is considered inconsequential.

Social content

     If this portrait seems altogether incoherent, that
is because it corresponds to a complex and incongruous
social reality: both portrait and reality are shaped
by the same forces, simultaneously operating. In her
brilliant and convincing study, The Feminization of
American Culture, Ann Douglas calls this process of
change in women's social and economic roles an
"economic disestablishment." Focusing her attention
on the first half of the nineteenth century, the 1820s
through the 1840s, she regards the process a by-product
of industrial development and mass factory production.
It was limited to a comparatively small section of
the American society - upper and middle class women in
the northeastern region of the United States. In other
areas and classes, whether married or single, women
continued their former roles and duties of domestic
manufacturers (especially in farming) or adapted to
new conditions, entering the labor market as factory
hands.[16]

The quickened pace of industrial production and railway transport introduced on the market a steadily growing amount of comparatively cheap and easily available goods which could and did compete successfully with home made and therefore often homely products. In the course of two generations the necessity diminished of carrying on domestic industries, ranging from candle and soap making to weaving and food preserving, while the old skills gradually disappeared. This process disrupted the balance between the two sectors of economic activity and, in consequence, undermined the long established roles of women in society. The change was perhaps more often felt than consciously realized. Yet there is evidence enough that at least some people perceived the true nature of the problem. As early as 1868, Mrs. C. F. Pierce discussed the position of middle class women with a surprising clarity of vision and understanding.

> But the entire class of women who keep
> servants - a class which is intelligent
> and refined . . . has sunk from its
> former rank of manufacturing producers
> to that of unproductive consumers, i.e.
> of persons who do not pay back in mental
> or manual labor an equivalent for the
> necessaries they use or luxuries they
> enjoy.[17]

On the economic level, industrialization deprived middle class women of their natural share in production which, until then, had been equal to men's, though separate. This fact, regarded by some as the principal defect of modern civilization, was considered by many a journalist the root of social disorder, suffering, and demoralization.

The social consequences of the process were complex but among the crucial changes was the polarization of American society into two opposing groups, sharing homes but otherwise moving in separate spheres. The world of men and the world of women were not just different; the gap between them, at least in the upper social strate, was widening rapidly, while distinctions were becoming more pronounced. In several respects the masculine role seemed easier to play, perhaps because it underwent fewer changes. His was the traditional part of an active and outgoing member of society, his primary responsibility being the material welfare of his family. Young men

entering adult life were offered the excitement and
adventure of business or professional competition with
all its challenges and dangers. Individual achievement was measured by the bank account, yet since
success was said to depend upon character, it imposed
the necessity of moral improvement.

Removed from immediate production, women found
their world shrinking and becoming marginal. Their
activities were confined to homes and society, their
diversions limited since adventure was considered
unsuitable for ladies. Their achievements, not
measurable in any objective currency, often seemed
precarious. Outside the arts, no improvement seemed
possible. Since the most highly valued feminine
attributes, innocence and virtue, were not acquired
but inborn, the best a woman could do in her life-
time was to perserve them intact. Conventional
thinking did not conceive of her moral improvement:
maturity led her, at best, toward knowledge and
consequent loss of innocence, but under less favorable
circumstances, to fall and sin.

Thus defined, social roles were frequently discussed in literary magazines. In 1875, Albert Rhodes,
the loading authority on social and society questions
of <u>Galaxy</u>, sought to justify the existing division.

> It has been his mission to work and to
> work hard, hers to be rather an object
> of luxury; his to contrive ways and
> means, hers to disburse . . . the man
> should always consider it a duty and
> a privilege to help the woman.[18]

Most probably unaware of the terms, Rhodes nevertheless perceives socio-economic reality as divided into
a base - the field of primary actions, essential for
survival which "naturally" belongs to man - and
secondary to it, a superstructure of culture, arts,
and ideas which had been claimed by women. His view-
point is essentially masculine, fully accepting the
status quo together with the ensuing distinctions
and obligations which extend far beyond responsibility
for the financial security of the family. Rhodes
fully shares the conviction argued a few years earlier
by Junius Henri Browne that, frailty being recognized
as woman's prerogative, man bears responsibility for
her conduct.

> Man and woman, though altogether equal,
> are so radically different. . . . Man
> being stronger and freer, ought to be
> superior. . . . Nature, fortune, society,
> and custom give him the advantage over
> his sister, to whom his relation is
> such that he must always be considered
> responsible for her. Her folly is usually
> traceable to his stupidity, and her
> errors are the result of his trans-
> gressions.[19]

Thus the desire to have woman sheltered at home is a
manifestation of his obligation to protect her; to let
her fall means to fail as a man.

The existing social order was further justified
by a psychological argument that woman finds her true
emotional satisfaction and human fulfilment primarily
as a wife and mother. Her essential wish and most
valued right is "to love and be loved." Assigning her
to domestic chores was not intended as restrictive,
but opening the most beneficial environment for her
growth and contentment. Browne insists that a wife
should be much more to her husband than a cook or a
housekeeper.

> She should have more than one side
> to her life . . . She may be a devoted
> wife and mother without forgetting that
> she was a woman before she was either. . .[20]

The general reluctance to let women do as they please
was further motivated by social interests. Its purpose
was to secure healthy children and their careful
upbringing which, being of primary importance to the
entire community, should take precedence over other
considerations. Discussing the question of co-
education, Oliver Wendell Holmes recognizes women's
claims to equality as legitimate yet instead of casting
his vote for their emancipation he carefully elaborates
the opposition between their individualistic demands
and far more crucial needs of society.

> It may be desirable that she should vote,
> but it is not essential to the tolerably
> comfortable existence of society. It
> is essential that she should be the
> mother of healthy children, well
> developed in body and mind. It is not

> essential that she should know as man
> knows, or produce by her ordinary labor
> as much as he does. It is essential
> that she should save her strength for
> the exhaustive labors which fall to her
> lot as a woman . . .[21]

In his concern for healthy children, Holmes does not
ban women to ignorance. To be intelligent companions
and mothers, girls must be educated as carefully as
the young men they are going to marry, but with due
regard to their future duties and fields of activity.
This demand for separate and differentiated education
served as an effective means of perpetuating the
existing division into masculine and feminine spheres.

Guarding jealously the exclusiveness of their own
world of business and the club, men were generous in
making concessions to women: granting fallacious
privileges and an ostensibly extensive field of
action. They seemed to recognize the fact that their
perennial preoccupation with business renders them
socially inferior to their wives and daughters.

> The woman of America is superior to the
> man in appearance as well as surface
> civilization: for the demands of his
> work are such that he cannot devote
> his time to the cultivation of graces
> in manner, language, and dress which
> she does.[22]

Whether by transfer or abandonment, culture and society
passed under the hegemony of women; many European
travellers and commentators ascribed the distinctive
character of American social life to the prominence
accorded to women. In the European tradition, the
arts, manners, and social exchange were considered
man's domaine as much as warfare, politics or manufacturing. Men of the aristocratic or court circles
dictated social rules and customs. Married women
played a decorative and entertaining but definitely
subordinate role while maidens were simply excluded
from social gatherings. In the age of the Founding
Fathers culture was as much the man's province in
America as it was in Europe. But by 1870, commentators
admitted that American society was family oriented,
with culture toned down or narrowed to amusements and
conversation suitable and comprehensible to young
girls. Hence, literature and art were censored on

their behalf; large areas of human experience, a good many current problems and events were never discussed in society. More strictly than in Europe inappropriate topics and gossips were banned to strictly male company which many found more congenial because free from restrictions in idiom as well as in manners imposed by the presence of "female innocents." The gulf separating the two groups was deepening.[23]

Women's response to the fact of this disestablishment was complex. To middle class women economic expansion and industrialization meant sudden changes of fortune, a more subtle stratification of society, and, possibly, new situations and tasks. Even if they observed its symptoms, few women realized the true nature of the process in which they were involved with the clarity of DeForest's description dated 1873.

> Mrs. Smiles . . . a dilapidated and
> tottering woman, was the entire support,
> financially and morally, of two healthy
> daughters. Because she was a relic of
> the time when ladies were not mere
> dandies; when work steadily done and
> responsibility loyally borne trained
> their characters into vigor when they,
> like their men, were producers as well
> as consumers.[24]

Characteristically for the masculine point of view, DeForest sees the fault in women; in feminine eyes men bear most of the blame.

> One might think men would reflect what
> they have done by their machinery in
> thus degrading women from the honorable
> rank of manufacturing producers into
> the dependent position of unproductive
> consumers, and seeing the exhaustive
> drain that such an army of expensive
> idlers must inevitably be upon society,
> that they would be glad to encourage
> them . . . to find new paths for their
> energies . . .[25]

However, traditional models of social roles did not encourage independence and self-reliance in women, nor were these qualities developed in the usual educational process. Therefore, unless some pressing need converged with an outgoing and forceful character, upper class women inclined to accept the role assigned to them while seeking psychological fulfillment in new areas and activities.

This embracing of new responsibilities was in fact a half-conscious reaction to the state of affairs which presented itself to most women. They perceived the man's world as active, expanding, and independent while their own seemed increasingly passive and static, if not narrowing down. To counteract the process, they tried to assume the role of initiators and modifiers of society life, devising patterns, codes and mechanisms of social usage and distinctions. At the same time, they sought to extend their range of activities into art, literature, and music, claiming the realm of ideas and refinement as their domain. Engaging in such novel pursuits American women depended largely on foreign examples. In Europe qualities of mind and art, leisure and affluence were ranked next to hereditary privileges and to engage in intellectual or artistic pursuits required no other justification but their intrinsic value; the inherent nobility of the task elevated the adept to a superior plane and granted him a higher social status. Thus, to American upper class women, rich in free time and money, Europe provided models of refined and sophisticated ways of spending both. It offered a more satisfying self-image, a sense of cultural mission as well as a social status equal to men's, in fact more advanced if less important for the economy of the country. It sanctioned widespread imitation of the elaborate and traditional European way of life which was regarded more pleasing than American simplicity and frankness. However, this expansion toward new goals, cultural achievements and social improvements was not freely and independently achieved, not "self-made." All these accomplishments depended, directly or indirectly, on money provided by fathers, husbands, and brothers.

Whether or not this financial dependence was felt as humiliating, ladies sought to re-establish the social balance by asserting their superiority and then demanding their due in homage, in obedience to etiquette, and of course, in money. Some, like Florence Howe Hall, well versed in all matters of savoir faire, considered this "specialization" only fair and sensible.

91

> In America our men are too busy to give
> their time to the consideration of social
> matters. Besides, women wish to rule,
> and the men of our country with the
> latter-day common sense that distinguishes
> them above all others think it only fair
> to grant us this privilege.[26]

Ladies of less serene temperament accepted their
dependence with a touch of vengeance: they disclaimed
business as low and vulgar. If we trust novelists of
the time,[27] many a wife made her husband earn what
she wished to spend. Man's duty was to provide a home
and secure its financial stability. Although the
master of his household, endowed by law, church, and
custom with absolute control over his family, he
exerted in fact little influence on domestic affairs.
These were managed in a sweet, obliging, yet
irresistible manner by his "better self", i.e. his
meek, patient, and loving wife. Paging through
literary magazines one occasionally comes across
short stories in which the wife silently submits to
her cold, inconsiderate, neglecting husband who
realizes his fault too late when the harm done by
his selfishness is beyond repair and the long
suffering woman is broken or dying. No chance of
atonement is offered to the repentent sinner. The
other variant of the same theme presents the man
humbled, repentant, begging forgiveness and mercy,
which may or may not be granted by the angelic
woman.[28]

The nineteenth century American woman recognized
the necessity to marry. A bad marriage seemed still
preferable to none at all. Many clever ones discovered they could carry out their will by persuasion,
maneuvering, coaxing and tears, thus reducing the
master-husband to an obedient, insignificant background
figure. His death, lamented in the properly tearful
manner was frequently a welcome relief, though no
woman-writer would admit the fact as openly as
John Hay.

> [Mrs. Belding] had been fond of her
> husband, but she had been a little
> afraid of him, and, when she wept her
> grief into tranquillity, she felt
> a certain satisfaction in finding
> herself the absolute mistress of her
> income and her bedroom. . . . she

> liked her breakfast at her own hours. . . .
> and she never met a man so fascinating
> as to tempt her to give up to him one
> of these rooms [i.e. closets adjoining
> her bedroom].[29]

A wealthy widow who could legitimately enjoy personal
and financial freedom as well as all the privileges
of a married woman, without the usual attending
restrictions and obligations, achieved a definitely
enviable position. Her satisfaction, however, was
carefully screened behind a more appropriate attitude
of gentle, docile acceptance of her lot. On the
conscious, spoken-about level, the validity of
marriage was never questioned. In such an atmosphere
Kate Chopin's The Awakening proved a novelty shocking
to the reading public of 1899. The novel deserves
attention for its literary merits: excellent character
drawing, unity of key images and symbols, sensitivity
to light, color, and texture, perfect harmony between
characters and incidents. The story of Edna Pontellier
is strictly personal, carrying no social implications,
although her case was probably more frequent than the
scandalized contemporaries cared to admit. Edna's
marriage, excellent to a casual observer, is a fairly
typical mixture of daily comforts, security, disappointments, customary compliance and frustrations.

> As the devoted wife of a man who
> worshipped her, she felt she would take
> her place with a certain dignity in the
> world of reality, closing the portals
> forever behind her upon the realm of
> romance and dreams.[30]

Accepting the role, she plays up to expectations well
enough, though she never becomes a "mother-woman"
idolizing her husband and children. Her actions are
to a large extent "prescribed" for her; yet, confined
by social ramifications, she retains a part that is
hers alone. Her awakening out of the socially defined
role to her true identity comes gradually.

> Mrs. Pontellier was beginning to realize
> her position in the universe as a human
> being, and to recognize her relations
> as an individual to the world within
> and about her.[31]

Her first instinctive rebellion is directed against being considered and treated as "a piece of valuable property" belonging to Mr. Pontellier, ever obliged to bend to his will. Edna comes to neglect her duties in all areas of her life - martial as well as social - because they are artificially imposed upon her and interfere with her newly discovered freedom. It takes her time to realize the true nature of the change: her love for Robert Lebrun stirs her sensuality long dormant under conventional propriety. The subtle yet expert hand of Alcee Arobin brings to the foreground all the instinctive needs and desires of aroused sexuality. Her passionate nature, too elemental to be repressed, grows to dominate her personality; denied fulfillment, it leads her to a suicide. From the point of view of the present considerations, The Awakening is unique. Kate Chopin focuses on the individual psyche of her heroine, disregarding any larger context of her actions. Like Edna, she skillfully eludes involvement in any particular social issue of her day. The shift to the inner, personal world marks the end of an era.

Throughout the final decades of the nineteenth century few fictional heroines experienced a comparable "awakening." Most novelists seemed reluctant to verge upon delicate topics of sensuality and sexuality. They considered personal needs and desires subordinate to the interests of society and disapproved of such an extreme individualism which threatened to dissolve social organization. Most lacked adequate language - metaphors and images as well as technique - to "translate" the problem into fictional situations, incidents, speech and thoughts. Thus, the nineteenth century heroines experience not an awakening but a change of heart. This ready-made, popular formula has been best defined by Gordon Kelly in Mother Was a Lady, his penetrating study of children periodicals between 1865 and 1890.

> The change of heart almost invariably
> proceeds from a moral state that
> varies from the merely inappropriate
> and embarrassing to one that is
> personally dangerous and socially
> vicious. . . . The key element in the
> formula . . . is a species of moral
> conversion, a dramatic shift in per-
> ception which combines a conscious
> recognition of the erroneous nature

94

of the individual's former behavior
with a conscious resolution to do better.
The change of heart is made manifest in
useful and appropriate activity following
the individual's conversion.[32]

The prodigals like Irene Lawrence (Amanda Douglas,
Hope Mills, 1879) and Christine Ludolph (E. P. Roe,
Barriers Burned Away, 1885) are essentially honest and
kind, but faulty education instilled in them false
notions of greatness based on wealth and birth. The
change of heart leads them to recognize the true
value and nobility of self-sacrifice, service and
duty: renouncing pride and selfishness, they grow
to self-knowledge and eventually find fulfillment
in love and marriage. Such a conversion was
frequently both ideological and religious.

     The general insistence that genuine culture
relies more upon qualities of character than superficial, external appearances echoes the parallel
efforts redefining success in terms of virtue
instead of one's bank account. In fact, the idea of
success permeated every sphere of American thinking.
Barred from economic competition, American middle
class women transferred the concept to their own
field of activity. Success, understood now as
social advancement, seemed as honorable and desirable
a goal as making a fortune or climbing to a prosperous
partnership. Writers who develop this theme, and
they are a majority, drew special attention to
conditions favoring such a career. By general consent
they all regard family background, character, and
proper marriage essential to woman's true progress.
The novelists take extra care to identify it with,
and make it dependent upon, the acceptance of strictly
defined norms and values. If Mrs. Job Grey, the
title character in Elle Williams' short story published
in Galaxy in 1871, becomes a brilliant leader of St.
Bo's (Boston?) society, it is "by sheer personal
influence among the best . . ." Inspired as a child
by a family story, she strove to improve herself, to
be a lady.

          From that time I strove to be like what
          this Marquise might have been; to
          make myself worthy to enter her imaginary
          presence and to touch her hand. You have
          no idea how miserably small were my
          first struggles toward refinement. I

                    have done almost everything that is honest
                    with these hands. I scorned nothing
                    which would lift me a hair's breadth
                    nearer the level of my beloved Marquise.[33]

Social success comes naturally in recognition and reward
for merit and nobility of the soul, unsullied by
mean desires. Like financial success to young
businessmen, social prominence is presented to young
ladies not as a goal to be pursued for itself, but as
a just and pleasant reward for proper conduct and
irreproachable character.

     A sudden rise to affluence and leisure through
her father's or husband's business success could open
new vistas of advancement before the heroine, the
aim which popular cliches presented as easily
attainable. William Dean Howells took up the problem
in his two major novels: in The Rise of Silas Lapham
and A Hazard of New Fortunes he considers the chances
of social success for the daughters of the newly rich.
The Lapham and Dryfoos girls are equally ambitious to
enter society. They are but vaguely aware that the
social elite is governed by countless minute rules
which they have no way of knowing. To a large extent
they remain blissfully ignorant of their own shortcomings and failures. Mrs. Mandel, a hired dame de
compagnie, can teach Christine and Belle Dryfoos the
basic precepts of good manners, yet, being an outsider
herself, she is unable to introduce them to New York
polite society. Besides, there is yet another
difficulty. Most attempts to emulate the upper
classes, if they are confined to external patterns of
behavior and have no correspondence in spiritual
(intellectual, artistic, emotional) refinement, turn
out simply ridiculous and embarrassing. To the
Coreys, the Laphams prove just "too much"; the
dinner party, comic in its disaster, remains the only
venture to introduce the self-made man into Boston
society. Margaret Vance's effort to be sociable to
the Dryfoos girls turns out most unsatisfactory to
both sides.

     Of the four heroines only Penelope Lapham enters
the upper class, and does it through marriage. It is
significant that Tom Corey becomes attracted by her
intelligence and personal qualities, remaining
indifferent to Silas' fortune and eventual bankruptcy.
Her social success, however, is questionable: the
Corey family accepts the young couple's departure for

Mexico with definite relief. Howells may have disapproved of close divisions and distinctions but knew
well enough their power and was too consciousness a
realist to contradict his own and his readers'
experience in the matter.

The combination of snobbish exclusiveness on the
one hand and crudity plus ignorance on the other
renders most attempts to cross class barriers futile.
Prudently indeed Howells carries his analysis no
further. His less skillful contemporaries tend to be
too insistent in their didacticism. Should one of
them write the story, he would make it plain that
Christine Dryfoos fails primarily because she imitates
the outer shape of good manners without embracing the
underlying value system and discipline. Secondly,
since passivity is essentially a feminine virtue, too
ardent a struggle to push upward contradicts woman's
very nature. In the nineteenth century view of the
problem woman's nature is to be a follower, not a
leader. Hence, in the true order of things, social
advancement, like love, should be offered to her by
a man.

The notion explains partly why "Cinderella"
stories appear but rarely in popular novels of the
period. Mary Wilkins Freeman's The Portion of Labor
(1901), is an example in which beautiful and intelligent
Ellen Brewster becomes a factory hand, giving up her
chance of going to Vasser, only to be "lifted up" at
the end of the novel by the young proprietor whom she
marries; but this dates from a later decade. Most
novelists seem to share a deeply rooted sense of
propriety in the matter. Any poor young man could
honorably love and aspire to marry a heiress, a lady:
becoming a gentleman he becomes worthy of her and
her love. Yet a similar aspiration was considered
degrading for a girl, unwomanly and unladylike. All
efforts to win man's favors, especially of one
superior in character or social status, are regarded
as either ridiculous or vulgar. John Hay's episode
in The Breadwinners (1884), in which Maud tries to
captivate the hero, a gentleman-millionaire offering
her his love and hand, is indeed as vulgar as it is
ridiculous.

The tremendous popularity of etiquette books in
the 1870s and 1880s indicates that a rise to
affluence was frequently accompanied by the ambition
of a parallel social advancement. The oracles on

propriety offered thorough instruction in all the
intricacies of polite conduct. They listed the
number, character and quality of one's wardrobe,
supplemented with details on time of day, season,
and occasion for which each item was worn. They
guided a beginner through the maze of afternoon calls,
visiting cards, ballroom and opera manners. They
settled doubts concerning respective duties of
various servants, proper use of the newly introduced
fork as well as the shape and cut of various wine
glasses. The etiquette books contain, first of all,
information necessary for those aspiring to a more
fashionable life style. Nevertheless, their
instruction goes deeper. The vivid, detailed, colorful descriptions are designed to impress and quicken
the reader's imagination; their purpose is to inform
about specific attributes like shape, color, and
material, conveying at the same time a sense of the
beauty, elegance, and aesthetic qualities enclosed
in refined objects and elaborate manners. As often
as not the writer includes a brief anecdote illustrating
a particular usage or inserts casually some
historical detail, a reference or a curiosity which
can be used as a "conversation piece." The uniform
consent declares that to be successful, to win favor
and recognition, courtesy and social refinement must
be rooted in respect for other people as well as one's
own dignity. Florence Howe Hall, one of the leading
authorities on social conduct, warns against superficial imitation of the externals.

> . . . the wealth of Midas would not long
> benefit the man who had not been taught
> to use it aright . . . wanting in all
> practical training and discipline . . .
> before one can rear a fair and comely
> superstructure of good manners, one
> must lay deep in the heart their
> necessary foundation, namely kindness
> and good will toward others, and due
> consideration for their feelings.[34]

With all the emphasis on elegance, taste, and
beauty of the fashionable circles, the etiquette books
confine their teaching to manners and customs of
society entertainment. They advise how to make good
conversation, what mistakes to avoid, but seldom do
they suggest suitable topics. Yet they do suggest
various menus appropriate for different occasions.
Cultivation and refinement are somewhat limited to

entertainment: to dinners, teas, balls, afternoon
calls. Matters pertaining to intellectual and
aesthetic appreciation seem left out of the picture.
Any reference to the arts is brief, though their
absence from the American social life is regarded a
deficiency. Highly experienced in society ways on
both sides of the Atlantic, Mrs. M. E. W. Sherwood
advised young men to lose no opportunity of self-
improvement.

> Works of art are a fine means of
> instruction. He should read and study
> in his leisure hours, and frequent picture
> galleries and museums. A young man
> becomes the most aggreeable of companions
> if he brings a keen fresh intelligence,
> refined tastes, and a desire to be
> agreeable into society.[35]

Within the next two pages, however, she admits that
books, art, and ideas are seldom discussed among
fashionable people; an evening at the opera is more
likely an occasion to display a new set of jewelry
than to enjoy music or judge the singers. Paging
through numerous novels of the period one observes
the same absence of intellectual and artistic interests
among the very best. There are a few exceptions -
Otto March (Queen Money) enjoys literature and initially
means to become a writer, yet gives up his ambition
for a more standard career in business. Lucy Florian
(the girl whom he is to marry at the end of the
novel) has a taste for books, good music, and
serious conversation which matches her distaste for
the glitter and rush of fashionable life. In Barriers
Burned Away (1885), E. P. Roe endows both characters
with artistic talents - Christine is an excellent
musician, Denis wins his reputation as a painter -
but both are marginal to the mainstream of Chicago
elite. So is Westover among Boston Brahmins in
Howells' The Landlord at Lion's Head (1897). In The
Age of Innocence (1920), Edith Wharton, who knew the
old New York of the 1870s intimately from the inside,
indicates that the two groups were equally unwilling
to associate with one another.

> Beyond the small and slippery pyramid
> which composed Mrs. Archer's world lay
> the almost unmapped quarter inhabited
> by artists, musicians and "people who
> wrote." These scattered fragments of

humanity had never shown any desire to
be amalgamated with the social structure.
Mrs. Archer . . . felt a certain timidity
concerning those persons. They were
odd, . . . perhaps . . . had gentlemanly
sentiments, but their origin, their
appearance, their hair, their intimacy
with the stage and the opera, made any
old New York criterion inapplicable to
them.[36]

In a society that had no inherited social distinctions
of rank and class, the exclusiveness of the
fashionable circles could not be maintained solely
by a high level of expenditure: this could be met and
bettered too easily by the emerging industrial
tycoons. The elite, defined and held together by
family ties, was protected by an elaborate set of
rules and precepts regulating the dos and don'ts of
the in-group. The familiarity with these minute,
ever-changing directives served as a letter of
recommendation without which one could hardly expect
to be recognized and accepted as an equal.

The novelists of the time actually use the term
"society" for two very different social groups, though
they seldom make the distinction clear. On the Eastern
seaboard, New York and Boston had a cooperatively
small, closely interrelated circles of long-settled,
well-to-do families. Their wealth, made in trade or
real estate some two generations earlier, was
respectably and securely invested to bring regularly
substantial dividends. Since idleness was considered
disreputable, men devoted their time to the legal
profession or banking, seldom engaging in doubtful
ventures of the stock exchange, never in politics.
Women followed the strictly prescribed routine of
winter seasons in town, summers in Newport or Saratoga,
interspaced with occasional trips to Europe, and
annual orders for the latest style wardrobe not to be
worn before two winters elapsed. To dress in the
current Parisian fashion signaled a definitely bad
taste, a subtlety seldom realized by the outsiders too
eager to show off and impress to keep their European
toilettes unpacked for two years. Such is the
exclusive Boston of Clare Kingsbury and Atherton in
Howells' A Modern Instance and the Coreys in The Rise
of Silas Lapham. This is also the New York of
Vanderwater family (E. O. Kirk's Queen Money),
Margaret Vance (A Hazard of New Fortunes) as well as

the van der Luydens and the Mingotts of The Age of
Innocence by Edith Wharton.

The exclusive "aristocratic" core as far as the
United States had anything like an aristocary, is
surrounded by a large circle of respectable yet
modest people who, whether related by marriage or
distant cousinship, do not presume to rank with their
betters at the top. This stratification seemed stable
and natural, accepted without ill feelings or self-
depreciation. However, it was seriously threatened
by newcomers who, trusting in their recently acquired
fortunes, strove to push their way among "the elect."
They usually fail to grasp the subtleties of the
social code which they violate unaware or careless
of the offence: they prove insensitive to the ruling
mores and customs, nor do they appreciate social
favors as favors but accept them as their due. The
novelists refer to this group too, especially to its
women, as society - sometimes causing additional confusion by presenting it as more dashing and stylish
than the subdued leisure class of inherited affluence.
What is important, however, is that writing about
either group the novelists carefully weigh wealth
against merit. They deplore luxury and display which
lend the unhealthy spirit of competition to social
intercourse. The few who can afford everything set
the standard of living and entertaining well above
the means of most. Thus, the young, self-made Chicago
society described by Henry Fuller in The Cliff-
Dwellers (1893) is run by a very small, smart set with
unlimited financial resources.

> They were half sisters . . . The Atwaters
> and the Ingleses ran as a kind of four-in-
> hand. The rich sister had married a poor
> man and the poor sister had married a
> rich man, and they all went along at
> the same pace. It was a somewhat
> rapid pace.[37]

Those who succumb to the allurements of expensive
tastes and amusements are soon drawn into a ceaseless
feverish whirl; deceived by the surface elegance of
the fashionable world, they fail to perceive its
superficiality, its sham brilliance, spiritual poverty,
ostentatious display and false values. To illustrate
the moral, Ellen O. Kirk presents how Arria White's
social ambitions overshadow her better self and sense.

> . . . they had become a fashionable
> couple. She was in a maelstrom of
> feverish ideas, wishes, and energies.
> She had counted on leisure and peace
> of mind . . . instead of which she
> felt more and more an incessant com-
> pulsion to press on to challenge
> admiration, to conquer by sheer force
> of energy. Formerly . . . her sole
> effort was to please a critical and
> fastidious husband. Nowadays he
> . . . had his own amusements and he
> seemed to take it for granted that her
> scheme of existence no more included
> him than his her.[38]

Engrossed in society life, Arria and Clayton grow
apart; furthermore, they neglect their duties and
responsibilities as parents. The death of little
Ethel is therefore both an outcome of and punishment
for parental default. Twain and Warner's The Gilded
Age (1884) contains another example: love of luxury
and prominence warp Laura's conscience and leads her
to morally questionable choices which include flirting,
lobbying, and an attempt at homicide.

Most novelists do not deny that social gaiety,
luxury and distinction can have a special charm.

> . . . to be the visible leader in her
> world, to be able to dispense a
> hospitality which should surpass any-
> thing heretofore seen . . . in a
> palace whose dimensions and splendor
> should awaken envy and astonishment -
> would this not be an attraction to a
> woman of imagination and spirit?[39]

The common objections are directed at the triviality
and the all absorbing power of such a life. Unaware
of danger, Margaret Henderson, the heroine of Charles
Dudley Warner's A Little Journey in the World (1889),
once a thoughtful, somewhat intellectual girl of
sensitive, discriminating conscience and high ideals,
yields and adapts herself to the insidious influence
of her milieu. Before the end of the story, she
submits to the surrounding materialism and learns to
compromise with its selfish morals and shallow gaiety,
becoming "a beautiful woman in all the success of
envied prosperity, with a dead soul."[40] To a large

extent Margaret remains unaware of her moral decline.
The realization of a comparable fall comes as humiliating to Bertha Amory (<u>Through One Administration</u> .
by F. M. Burnett, 1882), although it clearly results
not from any lack of rectitude, but an ardent desire
to meet her husband's wishes and expectations.

Both Margaret and Bertha are, in a sense, victims
of the changing patterns of American society. Their
elders and betters are either unaware of the fact that
the inflow of rich, influential businessmen lowered
the standards of social acceptability, or they feel
unequal to check their self-assured conquest of the
polite society. Hence, young and unexperienced girls
are left free to associate and fall in love with, and
marry men who prove totally unsuitable husbands.
Constrained by democratic feelings, their families
and friends do not even try to guard them against,
and then to dissuade them from, taking such a step.
Thus, the two reflect the painful dilemma of the
last quarter of the nineteenth century caught between
the old faith in human equality and perfectability
and the actual, levelling-down pressure of industrial
civilization.

In their efforts to expose evil, the novelists
seem to concentrate on major society sins, of which
ambition is, perhaps, most common. It is usually
accompanied by selfishness, greed, and vanity. Such
a combination of vices gives, Anna Madox, the heroine
of <u>John Andross</u> by Rebecca Harding Davis (1874), power
and the means to tempt, use, and destroy men. Her
haphazard upbringing failed to instill true values,
impose norms, and discipline temperament, while
sentimental stories supplied her with silly "heroic"
notions and vain ambitions. She may have "her poor
little brain filled with cheap romances and even as
a girl had a certain aptitude at assuming the role of
heroine in them;"[41] nevertheless she well knows how to
manipulate men's passions and weaknesses to her own
advantage, little caring for their moral downfall.
Selfish and calculating Anne eludes the consequences
of her deeds; she shifts the payment to men around
her. However shallow and silly, she is dangerous to
the existing moral and social order.

Rebecca Harding Davis was by no means the only one
to expose the pernicious influence of sentimental
fiction: DeForest, Twain, Harte, Eggleton and Howells
rebelled against prevailing tastes in the American

novel which reached their peak popularity in the mid-
century. Heart-breaking, tearful, and "lofty" tales
find a steady market among the less educated mass
public in any age; in 1866, however, when William
Dean Howells joined the editorial staff of The Atlantic,
sentimentality permeated the literary taste of
intellectual circles.

> Sentimentalism had risen from the
> popular depths and spilled its
> mawkishness over the entire American
> scene by 1860. . . . American
> literature had reached the state, by the
> outbreak of the Civil War, where the
> arbiter of its taste, the great
> Atlantic, spokesman for the culture
> of New England, and hence of the New
> World, had been invaded by sentiment-
> alism, stereotype and falsehood.[42]

As the editor of The Atlantic, Howells led the battle
against the sentimental and for realism in American
novel. His chief objection was the literary and
artistic mediocrity of the sentimental stories:
stereotyped characters, impossible situations,
incidents dominating characters, cliche phrases,
stilted, artificial language. The outline of the
latest favorite among Boston society ladies Tears,
Idle Tears which Howells builds into The Rise of Silas
Lapham, applies to the entire school.

> It's perfectly heart-breaking, as
> you'll imagine from the name; but
> there's such a dear old-fashioned
> hero and heroine in it, who keep
> dying for each other all the way
> through and making the most widely
> satisfactory and unnecessary
> sacrifices for each other. You
> feel as if you'd done them
> yourself.[43]

Discussing the novel Penelope Lapham judges the
romantic notion of self-sacrifice with her usual good
sense: to "give up" love and thus render three persons
miserable instead of just one is silly, unreasonable
and harmful. Yet, when, she becomes involved in a
comparable situation, she almost wrecks her own and
Tom Corey's happiness by following the fallacious
example.

In critical essays, book reviews, and his own
novels, Howells persistently attacked and ridiculed
sentimentality in the name of common sense and the
rational order of society. Since his criticism is
always mixed with satire, his heroes are never tragic:
their misadventures appear amusing even when their
stupidity is irritating. Alice Pasmer's heroics
(April Hopes, 1888) provide ample diversion to her
stormy courtship. Urged by an imperative sense of
duty on the one hand and impossibly high principles of
ideal conduct on the other, Alice can never relax into
peaceful contentment with actual, tangible happiness.
At every moment she enacts a part of some romantic
heroine, sublime in her self-sacrificing submissive-
ness. Yet, her self-conscious righteousness is, in
fact, narrow minded, ungenerous and selfish. She is
exacting and egotistic in her fanciful demands and
uncompromising to the point of obstinate rigidity.
Howells offers few excuses for his light-hearted,
careless and temporising Dan Maverick but judges him
leniently because his weaknesses are so human;
furthermore they are less harmful to individual and
social peace.

Howells' comic sense is best revealed in Indian
Summer, in which young, beautiful Imogene Graham sets
out on a sentimental venture to "make up" to a middle-
aged man, Colville, for a shattered love of his youth.
The noble mission blinds her to the differences
between them in age, interests, habits, likes and
dislikes. Her infatuation flatters him to play the
role of a much younger bachelor, and for herself also
to believe she really loves him. He feels obliged
to act according to her imaginings and expectations
against his better judgment: to let her realize how
she has deceived herself and consequently put herself
forward would hurt and humiliate her. To spare her the
pain of such a discovery, he proposes a marriage
which is bound to end in disaster. Colville's position
of a middle-aged lover becomes all the more ridiculous
because he constantly tries to attract and please Mrs.
Bowen, an old friend acting as Imogene's chaperone.
What he fails to realize is that he loves her and not
her young charge. Howells heightens his comedy and
criticism in the final part of the novel. An
accident shocks enough common sense into Imogene and
Colville to break their engagement but sentimentality
continues to distort human relations. Feeling guilty
and humiliated to have loved him while he was engaged
to Imogene, Mrs. Bowen belives it a valid reason for

refusing to marry him. It takes a child, Effie, to
settle this confused affair to everybody's satisfaction.
In the nineteenth century sentimental fiction neither
plots, nor characters, nor language reflected contemporary reality in the slightest degree; the image
of life they offered was altogether false and so were
the manners and morals they commanded. To the sober,
practical minds of the later nineteenth century the
influence of sentimentalism disseminating false ideas
about life, devotion, duty and noble conduct appeared
highly dangerous to social order and stability. If
such notions were to prevail and actually guide human
affairs, they would inevitably lead to much misery,
folly and chaos. The danger seemed possible enough
when one considered the enormous popularity of these
books serving as educational models for many young
girls who lacked better mental and spiritual guidance.

Howells' attack on sentimentalism indicates his
sincere, though maybe naive, belief in the power of
books to shape reality to influence man's thinking
and mold his behavior. Like many contemporary guidebooks for young girls, his criticism advocates rational
and workable solutions to complexities of human and
social affairs. To fulfill its educational function
the novel should balance the representation of reality
as it is with a clear vision of what it should be.
The reading public probably cared for entertainment
more than for the most gently implied didacticism,
yet expected and accepted it as obvious and necessary.
The moral message justified in a way those parts of
the novel dwelling on wickedness, evil, folly, misery
and sin - the entire unpleasant side of the contemporary existence. Absence of a moral point of
view became the chief objection against naturalistic
fiction. Conversely, most inadequacies of American
realism - its reticence, taboos, lack of daring, mild
passions, middleclass propriety, and happy endings -
result from the obligation to uphold ethical standards
of judgment. If today we are often impatient with
various shortcomings of American realistic fiction it
is perhaps because we no longer share its preoccupation
with moral and social order.

However, the entire generation born in the
agrarian, antebellum world, the generation reaching
maturity around the Civil War faced urban and
industrial America overwhelmed, if not bewildered,
by the change. Individual response could vary from
sorrow, regret and nostalgia to the most unconditional,

106

enthusiastic optimism; nevertheless, all shared the
experience of living in a flux. The familiar places
disappeared, old customs and usages vanished, the
well established order lost its validity while norms
and values no longer seemed relevant. In an
increasingly fragmented society all the more attention
was given to home and family, which were continually
presented as a stable and unchanging haven. In his
Decline of American Gentility, Stow Persons suggests
that the traditional image of the family which
dominates novels of the period actually reflects an
earnest effort to find some "immovable point in the
whirling universe."

> While such traditional institutions
> as class, church, and stable community
> life crumbled under the impact of the
> mass society Americans fell back upon
> the home as their last refuge and
> support.[44]

Two institutions alone at the extreme ends of social
organization, the family and the Union, seemed to
function in the general chaos of change. Indeed they
were endowed with special symbolic, almost religious
meaning because they contained hope for continuity,
stability, security as well as some rational social
existence.

Persons' earlier comment that "Howells stubbornly
refused to recognize the signs of family transfor-
mation"[45] is valid for a greater part of the
respectable journalism and fiction dealing with the
subject in the last quarter of the nineteenth century.
In the post-Civil War years the social and intellectual
elite was highly concerned about the growing number
of divorce cases accepted with relaxed tolerance by
public opinion. This change of attitude reflected a
profound and disturbing shift in moral perception.
The fervent debate on divorce revolved around the
basic question of the purpose and function of marriage.
Among those writing for the more conservative
magazines like The Atlantic and The Century, few
advocated emancipation of women, though some recognized
the necessity of new legislation concerning married
women and their right to own and manage personal
property. A gradual decline of protestant theology
and rigorous moral control converged with the
widening circulation of new social theories of
J. S. Mill and Herbert Spencer. In the new

107

philosophical climate marriage was no longer regarded
as a social estate but as a contract between two
individuals, an agreement defining mutual rights and
obligations which could be dissolved at any moment by
the consent of the interested parties. Defending
the traditional model of the family, Henry James, Sr.
argued, in his two articles "The Woman Thou Gavest
With Me" and "Is Marriage Holy?" published in The
Atlantic in 1870, for the social and spiritual
dimension of love and marital union which could
develop only when guaranteed security and permanence.

> [Mr. Mill] regards marriage as a mere
> voluntary tie between men and women,
> essentially devoid of social obligation,
> or having at most only a politico-
> economical interest to society. . . .
> Now the marriage institution does not
> originate in the necessities primarily
> of this or any other man or woman, but
> in the necessities of society itself.
> It is a strictly social institution,
> growing out of the exigencies, not of
> human nature, but of human culture . . .[46]

Reviewing the problem for The Century twelve years
later, Washington Gladden lists among the chief causes
which collaborate to desintegrate the family new
social theories, agitation on behalf of woman suffrage,
and extreme individualism.

> In the exaltation of the individual,
> modern society has greatly weakened the
> family bond. The feelings of mutual
> obligation and fidelity have been
> suppressed in the assertion of personal
> liberty.[47]

Galdden argues for a more stringent divorce law which
would, on one hand, discourage irresponsible, rash
marriages, and tighten economic ties by identifying
economic interests in joint ownership of property.
He is fully aware that legislation provides but half-
measures; nevertheless law is the only guard against
forces undermining the sacredness and permanence of
the family, i.e. of social organization. However
impotent to eradicate evil, law can effectively protect society by hampering such processes that threaten
its integrity and stability.

Under the present economic system we
find wealth rapidly accumulating in
the hands of a few men, and great
multitudes sinking into pauperism.
That tendency does not seem to us
wholesome; we point to it as evidence
that there is something wrong in our
economic system. Similarly, when we
see divorces steadily increasing, we
need not assume that the movement is
in the direction of the ultimate
social order; it may be a temporary
reaction toward social anarchy and
corruption.[48]

Gladden's brief commentary seems particularly interesting. Comparing new tendencies in social mores
with those observable in economy, he touches the
heart of the matter. Principles governing both
were affected by the new concepts and values
concerning man and society; consequently, changes
occurring in both are traceable to the common source.
Extreme individualism and the impact of social
Darwinism redefined many affairs once regarded as
lying in public domain now as private and personal -
and hence free from public responsibility. In the
man's world of business the diminished social control
helped to evolve monopolistic strategies and new
business ethics independent of traditional Christian
morality. At the same time this loosened control
upset the harmony of the woman's realm, opening new
perspectives of education, profession, financial
independence and suffrage, without adjusting, however,
any of her former duties and obligations as wife,
mother and homemaker.

American fiction of the period accurately records
changes which new social thought and new conditions
wrought in traditional patterns of married life and
relations. A closer look at several novels focused
on marital crises indicates that the awareness of
change, experienced more frequently as a deterioration
than an improvement, motivated many a novelist to
defend social order and to advocate control. Without
depreciating individual achievements, they reassert
the value of training and discipline superimposed on
natural human impulses. Howells, who consistently
recognized the priority of social over personal
interests, was perhaps the most outspoken on the
subject. In A Modern Instance (1881) he makes

Atherton, a prominent Boston lawyer, pronounce opinions
to a large extent his own.

> The natural goodness doesn't count. The
> natural man is a wild beast, and his
> natural goodness is the amiability of
> a beast basking in the sun when his
> stomch is full. . . . No, it's the
> implanted goodness . . . - the seed
> of righteousness treasured from
> generation to generation, and
> carefully watched and tended by
> disciplined fathers and mothers in
> the hearts where they have dropped
> it. The flower of this implanted
> goodness is what we call civilization
> . . .49

Like Henry James, Sr., Howells regards marriage a
public affair, an indispensable element of social
organization upheld by a conscious and willing
obedience to the established rules and norms. All
members owe allegiance to the cultural code of society
but those whom wealth, family background, or education
place in the higher ranks bear special responsibility
to support the established social structure. If the
vulgar, ignorant, and uncultured reject norms and
trample upon conventions, their misbehavior,
disastrous to their immediate associates, remains a
regrettable yet marginal exception to general
conformity. The very same deed, however, becomes a
serious offence if committed by someone of the elite.
Then, it becomes an act of defiance disrupting
social order and questioning its meaning and validity.

Such a conviction provides Atherton with arguments
for his prolonged discussion with Ben Halleck on
marriage and divorce. The novelistic formula that all
who obey the generally accepted rules and follow the
prescribed mode of behavior grow happy and rich,
expresses and conforms the very same belief in the
ultimate value of the given social code. Hence,
continuing folk tradition, popular novels trace many
marital troubles to improper conduct before or during
the engagement; or, in a more frequent variant of the
plot ending with a wedding, disregard for conventional
propriety augurs misery and disaster in the couple's
life together. Thus, to a careful reader of the day,
the very first chapter of A Modern Instance contains
the germ of later troubles for Marcia Gaylord and

Bartley Hubbard. On parting after an evening spent
together Bartley kisses the girl; infatuated, Marcia
neither resists nor resents this intimacy which
society's conventions permitted infrequently and only
after the engagement. Her father's stern inquiry
brings her out of a happy reverie - ashamed for his and
her own sake, she realizes that Bartley actually made
no such promise. In love at the very first sight,
Marcia was never able to hide her feelings. When
engaged, she expresses her love freely, without the
hesitation or reserve generally expected of "nice"
girls. Her education failed to discipline her
tempestuous temperament; later on, ambition and pride
proved insufficient to restrain her jealousy and
passion. Faced with Bartley's departure from Equity,
she once more defies the conventions: asking his
forgiveness she accepts immediate marriage and
leaves with him for Boston.

Bartley's faults against propriety are just as
serious. Easy-going, selfish, and vain, he is ready
to flatter and pay compliments to every pretty girl
in the village, primarily for the sake of pleasure
and amusement. He finds his carefree bachelorhood
too comfortable to get entangled in a serious affair.
His engagement to Maria occurs unintentionally as he
imprudently speaks the magic key phrase "I love you;"
so when Marcia breaks their engagement in a fit of
jealous anger, he accepts the fact with genuine relief
mixed with some regret. He does not appreciate love
which he never worked to win: therefore, when the
initial sexual attractiveness passes, he becomes bored
and tired of the entire affair of his marriage.

In the first two years of their marriage Marcia
grows to realize the destructiveness of her passionate
temper, her possessiveness and jealousy. Recognizing
deficiencies of her own up-bringing which gave too
much freedom to her natural inclinations, she intends
to train her daughter in moral and social discipline.
Yet the new understanding avails her little and her
earnest efforts to exercise some self-control prove
ineffectual. Bartley's selfishness, bent on immediate
gratification, is guided by no principle, moral or
social, for abstract notions of honor, dignity, respect,
and order carry little meaning for him. Ben Hallek's
brief outline of his character is mercilessly accurate.

He was a poor, cheap sort of a creature.
Deplorably smart and regrettably

111

> handsome. A fellow that assimilates
> everything to a certain extent, and
> nothing thoroughly. A fellow with no
> more moral nature than baseball. The
> sort of chap you'd expect to find, the
> next time you meet him, in Congress
> or the house of correction.[50]

Of the two, Bartley is perhaps more dangerous to
social stability. His selfishness appears good-
natured but, in fact, becomes the force disrupting
family life and, by doing so, undermines the established
social order.

A Modern Instance offers a penetrating analysis of
the gradual disintegration of the Hubbard marriage
caused by psychological make up and character
deficiencies of both. Significantly enough, Howells
illustrates the process presenting his characters in
their social roles. Bartley's moral decline is
depicted through his journalistic career while Marcia
is seen primarily as a wife, to a lesser extent as a
mother. Outlining their story, Howells repeatedly
emphasizes that, by yielding to their spontaneous,
instinctive impulses, they both violate the fundamental
precepts regulating human relations. Carried away by
emotions, they hurt and humiliate one another with
such perfect accuracy of aim that long intimacy
ensures sparing no pain. From the point of view of
manners and civilized politeness they both act as
savages and barbarians.

Isolated from fixed social ramifications and
lacking economic security the Hubbard marriage offered
a precarious chance of stability. To a casual observer
the Hubbards appear civilized enough, though Marcia's
manners bear the stamp of rustic simplicity and
Bartley's superficial refinement hardly covers his
essential crudeness. Their good manners, however, are
superficial, leaving their hearts and thoughts coarse.
If they are frank and outspoken, Howells finds their
spontaneity of dubious value; unless guided by genuine
refinement, by constant earnest concern for others, it
is indeed an unpredictible spontaneity "of a wild
beast" threatening peaceful and harmonious co-existence.

In his last completed novel The Golden Bowl (1904),
Henry James depicts a comparable marriage crisis. Of
the four characters involved, Maggie Verver is the only
one who married for love. Her feelings for the Prince,

as possessive as Marcia's, do not loosen, however, her former emotional ties with her father. Wishing to keep her new passionate love as well as the old tender intimacy she avoids the decisive choice; act, which places both men in false positions, leads Adam Verver to a "marriage de convenance" for the sake of his daughter's peace of mind, and the Prince to a renewed intimacy with Charlotte. Therefore, it is Maggie's task to re-establish the moral order in the two marriages.

The mutual absorption of the Ververs presents their entering into truly personal relations with their respective spouses. Additionally, Maggie, fascinated by the past, perceives in her husband, Amerigo, a personality - the prince rather than a person. He is the most valuable possession among their accumulated treasures, an exquisite collection item. Similarly Adam fails to appreciate Charlotte as an individual. In his very offer he treats her instrumentally: as his wife she is to ensure Maggie's happiness. Under such circumstances the Amerigo-Charlotte romance seems inevitable for deeper reasons than their former passionate affair. In a way, it is bound to happen because they are constantly thrown together by the self-preoccupied Ververs who only ask to be left alone. Yet there are other forces at play. Both Amerigo and Charlotte consider their respective "marriages de raison" as bi-lateral contracts binding them to fulfill accepted obligations. They both diligently and loyally adhere to their formal agreements: they represent the Ververs' wealth and artistic collection to the best advantage. From their point of view their liaison involves no betrayal since legal contracts are not subject to moral evaluation.

Discovering the truth Maggie faces the crucial problem how to separate lovers without marring the personal integrity of all concerned: Adam's innocence, Amerigo's perfection, Charlotte's talents. She realizes that to win her husband she must meet his high aesthetic standard. Simple and straightforward, she chooses the indirect way of silence and perfect composure which cannot fail to win his respect, leaving him the time and freedom to adjust and develop a new moral sense, without violating his integrity. At the same time, she strives to protect Adam, to hide from him the enormity of guilt, falsehood, betrayal, and ingratitude.

It was extraordinary: they positively
brought home to her that to feel about
them in any way of the immediate,
inevitable, assuaging ways, the ways
usually open to innocence outraged and
generosity betrayed, would have been to
give them up, and that giving them up was,
marvellously, not to be thought of.[51]

Her love, even for Charlotte whose influence over her
father, and keen perception and skill at manipulating
people she greatly fears, makes all thought of revenge
or even just punishment impossible. It carries her
further to accept the burden and pay the ultimate
price of separation from her beloved father.

With Amerigo she claims to know everything yet
refrains from exerting the slightest pressure by word
or gesture, thus leaving him completely free to decide
his course. Toward Charlotte, she adopts a diametrically different policy: honest and truthful,
Maggie lies without hesitation or doubt. She denies
all consciousness of any harm done, but turning the
tables, confesses guilt never committed or intended.
This delicate maneuvering goes on amidst the leisure
and comforts of Adam's country residence all summer
long. Except for a single confrontation over the
broken golden bowl, there are no scenes, no accusations,
no harsh words. No one admits or confesses any sin.
On the contrary, amidst tension, suspicion, shame and
anguish, all four characters behave with scrupulous
politeness, gracious cordiality and perfect manners.
They watch one another closely, read signs and gestures,
interpret words, looks, and tone of voice but nothing
is brought to the surface. This admirable reticence
and self-control are, in fact, the highest proof of
genuine refinement.

Half way through the summer, Maggie gains a deeper
understanding of the drama in which they are all
involved, the awareness which opens for her the
possibility of choosing her part in it.

Spacious and splendid, . . . it was a
scene she might people, by the press
of her spring, either with serenities
and dignities and decencies, or with
terrors and shames and ruin, things
as ugly as those formless fragments
of her golden bowl she was trying so

hard to pick up.[52]

The issue at stake is more valuable, more vital than
her personal happiness and her marriage. It is the
choice between serenity and terror, dignity and shame.
Maggie persistently strives to spare their self-respect
and dignity. Her deceptions and lies cannot alter the
truth, but sparing pain and humiliation they allow
them all to "pick up the broken fragments," and go on
living together.

    Narrating Maggie's subtle and skillful maneuvers
James repeatedly emphasizes her self-possession.
She achieves her goal because she is able to master
her instinctive, elemental reactions and act with
intelligence and consistency, the two accomplishments
her husband watches with growing admiration. This
admiration for the high art of living Henry James,
as Dorothea Krook comments, must definitely have
shared.

> For there is a beauty . . . in reticence,
> composure and civility inflexibly main-
> tained, with every appearance of natural-
> ness and ease, when the heart is being
> torn to pieces by anguish, terror, and
> himiliation; and though the over-
> civilized - the Edwardian England for
> instance - had perhaps too much of it,
> the under-civilized - James' simpler
> Americans - had too little; and James
> himself . . . would not have chosen
> to live among the more civilized
> rather than the less if he had not seen
> its beauty as well as its ugliness.[53]

In his evaluation of social conventions James considers
both sides of the coin. Faultless decorous behavior
may mask duplicity, selfishness and corruption,
occurrences he himself exposed in his earlier novels.
Nevertheless, scrupulous obedience to this artificial
code can smooth frictions inevitable in human encounters and mercifully cover up one's failures, weaknesses, and sins. Thus, social conventions are the
product of civilization, an art of living with
"serenity, dignity, and decency" under any circumstances.

    Edith Wharton's New York society as depicted in
The Age of Innocence, in which she was born and brought

up in the 1860s and 1870s, was governed by conventions as strict as those of James' international circles though more narrow-minded and stifling. That static, orderly world is ruled by "taste" and "form," the conformity to which is kept under surveillance primarily by family women. Occasional scandals and compromising affairs, usually termed "unpleasant," are never faced openly, nor even spoken about, but long training in watching and interpreting the words and actions of others proves sufficient to handle most embarrassing situations.

> In reality they all lived in a kind
> of hieroglyphic world where the real
> thing was never said or done or even
> thought, but only represented by a
> set of arbitrary signs.[54]

According to the custom, the shift in Newland Archer's allegiance is met by a silent solidarity of the entire family: Ellen's name and affairs are never mentioned in his presence. Their silence forbids his asking questions; furthermore it quietly but effectively separates the two.

Innocent to the point of what seems ignorance, May immediately senses the change in Newland's love and views, and, never letting him or anybody know her suspicion, she silently strives to keep him. She plays her game of deceptions masterly for one apparently so simple and straightforward. On the one hand she maneuvers things so that her husband's relations with Ellen appear the reflection of her own, his services and attentions seemingly performed at her wish, with her knowledge and approval. On the other, she skillfully forestalls his taking any radical, irrevocable step or, for that matter, saying anything which would disturb the surface harmony of their existence. Fully aware of the impending crises, she plays her only card with an expert hand, counting on the essential uprightness and sense of responsibility of both. The news of her pregnancy sends Ellen back to Europe and prevents Newland from breaking up their marriage to follow her across the Atlantic. Her announcements, made to each separately at the decisive moment, could hardly be timed more adroitly.

His unusual love affair with Ellen Olenska becomes for Newland an experience similar to that of Edna Pontellier's in Kate Chopin's The Awakening (1899).

Even before meeting her, he realized the limitations
and superficiality of his world closed to broader
ideas, arts, imagination and free expression of mind
and heart, yet accepted and, up to a point,
respected them. Through his love for Ellen he dis-
covers the possibility of a much larger, freer way of
living which could satisfy his emotional, intellectual,
and artistic needs, long stifled and starved in the
rigidly controlled, complacent and boringly monotonous
New York. If he yields to family pressure and
expectations, it is not through lack of will or
courage. At the very bottom of his heart he accepts
and appreciates the values which social conventions
protect, he consciously pays his price for the
"serenity, dignity, and decency" of human relations
and social order.

> He had been . . . "a good
> citizen." . . . His days were full,
> and they were filled decently. He
> supposed it was all a man ought to ask.

> Something he knew he had missed:
> the flower of life. . . . Their long
> years together had shown him that it
> did not so much matter if marriage was
> a dull duty, as long as it kept the
> dignity of a duty: lapsing from that,
> it became a mere battle of ugly
> appetites.[55]

In the New York of the Mingotts and the van der Luydens,
society's conventions become the means of manipulating
its members to ensure their conformity, repressing the
weaker and expelling the uncontrollable rebels.

Newland Archer is not a ragged Huck Finn who,
finding civilization too confining and cruel, ruled
by hypocrisy, violence, and injustice can "light out
for the Territory." No such escape to the "Territory"
or Europe is possible for him. Edith Wharton carefully balances positive against negative effects of
rigorous social control. In retrospect, Newland
himself seems unable to choose between the old and the
new mode of existence. "After all, there was good in
the old ways," but his reflection is soon followed by
another: "there was good in the new order, too."[56]

If Huck Finn expresses the enterprising, optimistic
individualism of the nineteenth century, Newland Archer

117

becomes its sober and better socialized counterpart.
In the 1880s the world of antebellum, rural South of
Mark Twain's boyhood did not exist any more; John
Rockefeller's remark, "individualism is gone, never
to return," seems to apply as well to other areas of
experience beside business. In the last quarter of
the century we can observe a gradual increase in
social conformity accompanied by a parallel shift
of emphasis from individual to community interests.
The process was assisted by a more general tendency
toward uniformity and standardization. Ideologically,
it fed on the Victorian notions of propriety and
respectability, drawing some support from the
social thought of the Age of Reason. Such old-
fashioned concepts, however, remained marginal to the
mainstream of American thought which was increasingly
dominated by the theory of evolution. Therefore,
before the century was over, popular feelings reversed
to individualism again - choosing Theodore Roosevelt,
Norris' business tycoons, Richard H. Davis' and Jack
London's "supermen" as their heroes.

The Age of Innocence depicts a well established
elite of leisure and unostentatious expenditure,
resolved to preserve its exclusiveness. Toward the
end of the century, however, this old "aristocracy"
was rapidly becoming marginal and insignificant for
the main current of events. In this society, defined
and ruled by conventions, it was assumed that a
marriageable girl knew nothing of actual life, had
no past and no experience, so that she could offer her
husband a beautiful, blank page to fill as he pleased.
Sheltered throughout her life, May Welland Archer
seemed content enough with her limited existence: she
had all she could wish for. Furthermore, she lacked
imagination or intellectual curiosity to venture outside her confined circle. Yet many girls in her
position, and the multitude of less fortunate ones,
found the futility of such existence hard to bear.
Numerous fictional heroines complain that their too
narrow field of usefulness renders their lives petty
and shallow, while men's chivalric complicity of
silence bars womankind from information and understanding. Robert Grant, who sketched the situation of
society girls with much sympathy, regarded this
enforced ignorance as the root of much evil.

Existence was not easy for women. What
a feeble, insignificant part, after all

> those in her condition played in the
> struggled of life! How little
> opportunity they had of understanding
> its real workings! . . . They had to
> be dependent for information on what
> men saw fit to tell them; and were
> they not victims of delusion, in
> consequence? . . . Certain opinions
> and conditions of affairs were to be
> assumed as true in their presence
> which every man believed to be false.[57]

Robert Grant was not a reformer. Wishing for a more
definite purpose in life, Dorothy Crosby, his heroine
in An Average Man (1884), shrinks from the combative,
self-asserting spirit of the feminists.

> She recoiled instinctively from all ideas
> of invading man's province, and
> assimilating what was masculine. . . .
> She could not but call to mind the
> unpleasing qualities of the female
> advocates of a change in the status
> of women. . . she felt an intuitive
> hostility toward everything that would
> conduce to sully or impair her woman-
> liness.[58]

She remains faithful to her better self to be amply
rewarded for her virtue and patience in love and
prosperity.

In more popular novels such complaints are
usually accepted as valid, and gain the writer's
sympathy. Occasionally the novelists draw attention
to the prevailing attitudes which hamper woman's
personal development, stressing that ignorant of the
basic facts of business, she is likely to fail in her
crucial duty: in guiding her husband's moral choices.
The turns of the plot by which the heroine leads her
husband to a financial embarassment because she has
no idea of his income were favorite stock situations
in popular novels of the day. They served, it seems,
several purposes. They formed the ground for the
dramatic and psychological conflict which could range
from sudden bankruptcy to serious estrangement between
husband and wife, to moral struggle for the
protagonist's integrity. Such problems, well familiar
to the reading public after the Civil War, lent an air
of credibility to the fictional world and characters.

At the same time they offered an opportunity to voice the writer's opinion on the woman question.

In the final quarter of the nineteenth century the situation of women, their position and role in society which Henry James considered "the most salient and peculiar point in our social life," attracted much attention and discussion. Those who perceived the consequences of industrialization and economic dis-establishment urged the necessity of some fundamental change, but few could suggest a positive and acceptable direction of reform. They realized that, lacking a profitable and useful occupation, well-to-do women turned either to frivolities of society play and competition, or grew restless, resentful and dis-content. As "expensive idlers" they were a heavy financial burden on society. The harm done was both economic and moral. Many journalists and readers were concerned with the plight of women, unmarried, orphaned or widowed, forced to earn their living. The frequent ups and downs of the national economy and even more frequent reversals of individual fortunes could make self-support a necessity for any woman. Thus, to prepare her against such a misfortune seemed imperative, but it required a fundamental change of attitude toward labor, too often regarded undesirable and even shameful. The other measure recommended was to amplify girls' education with practical training in some vocation, suggestions varying from book-keeping and typewriting to dentistry and nursing. Made in 1888, they are all the more significant because ten years earlier, in the mid 1870s, women were encouraged to learn the skills which would allow them to earn an extra income while remaining at home.[59]

A parallel shift was occurring in the attitude toward marriage. Without questioning its function, journalists tended to view it in a new perspective of equality. As early as 1871 Henri Junius Browne claimed that a wife should be her husband's friend, helpmate, and mistress. Characteristically, he never considered her role in the larger world outside her family. L. E. Holman's letter to the editor of The Century, December 1888, marked the distance which at least a part of the society had travelled.

> Do not bring them [young girls] up to
> believe that marriage is the aim of
> a woman's life any more than it is
> of a man's or that it is more honorable

and dignified than work.[60]

The more respectable, conservative magazines
like The Atlantic preferred not to become involved
in controversial issues like women's rights and
emancipation. Hence, they sooner discussed points of
secondary importance, voiced well-balanced, liberal
opinions and never reported conspicuous careers or
the heated debates of the feminists. Occasional
reports of women's successful ventures in independence
aim to show that women lack no mental or moral
qualities necessary for success, but are fully capable
of coping with work and business in case of need.

The position of a novelist regarding the
suitability or propriety of women's careers was perhaps
even more precarious. His audience was composed
largely, some insist predominantly, of women whose
opinions, tastes, and prejudices he had better take
into account. Most writers avoided the problem
altogether; not more than a handful of middle class
novel heroines earn their living, those who do it by
choice are fewer still, and seldom with the author's
approval. On the other hand, the working class girls
do, as they should, work to help support their
families, as well as to keep out of mischief, until
they are married and provided for. The popular
novelists present women's work and money-earning
as a sad necessity, at best borne with the fortitude
and serenity of exemplary Alice Norwell in Thomas
Stewart Denison's An Iron Crown (1885). They use this
trial to test character, to reveal latent qualities
of their heroines. Joseph Kirkland finds with Anne
Sparrow, in Zury, the Meanest Man of the Spring County
(1887), that her determination and perseverence to win
security for her children is admirable, and yet
deplorable. Kirkland's unequivocal, if unpronounced,
judgment is that the struggle for a living is not a
fit undertaking for a woman. In the natural and proper
course of events security and comforts should be
provided by her husband.

The only case of a girl's success story, i.e her
rise from financial and social mediocrity to affluence,
is included as a subplot into Henry Fuller's The Cliff-
Dwellers (1893). Cornelia McNabb is, in fact a
genteel, socially acceptable variant of Sister Carrie,
only seven years her junior. On coming to Chicago,
Cornelia begins as a servant girl but, using intelligence and energy, she learns new skills of shorthand

and typewriting and soon gains a satisfying and renumerative occupation. All in accordance with the Horatio Alger formula, a happy marriage to a millionaire's son and heir rewards her efforts at self-improvement.

The popular formula identifying women with home has its exceptions in the late nineteenth century novels. The first example coming to mind is Henrietta Stockpole, the energetic, opinionated, and on the whole successful lady-correspondent in The Portrait of a Lady. Yet James is hardly concerned with her professional duties and career. He provides only such scarce information on this point as thorws light upon her personality and her relation to the heroine. A minor figure in the plot, Henrietta serves as a foil to Isabel because by temperament, education, profession and personal choice she is not a lady. Nor will she become one on marrying an English gentleman. Indeed, few writers of the period, if any, denied the intellectual capacity of at least some women for learning, yet they all shared the conviction that public life requires physical, nervous and mental exertion beyond the ordinary strength of womanly constitutions. Therefore, they regard any attempt or ambition to enter such a strain and competition as obviously misguided and foolish. In The Gilded Age Mark Twain and Warner's heroine, Ruth Bolton, studies medicine, a project which the authors refuse to take seriously. Her girlish whim, though well-intentioned, involves merely a waste of time, effort, and money, for as soon as she falls in love she gives up her ambition for the true calling of a wife and mother. William Dean Howells' analysis of the problem is more thorough and penetrating. With true New England earnestness Grace Breen, a homeopatic doctor, enters upon her duties (Dr. Breen's Practice, 1881) only to find herself unequal to the task. Her feminine qualities, emotionality, even her grace and womanly softness interfere with the demands of her profession which requires a masculine clarity of mind, quick decisions and firm will. Torn by conflicting emotions she finds peace and refuge in the total surrender of marriage. Only then, fortified by her husband's protection, can her knowledge be usefully employed in caring for the children of his employees.

However strongly the novelists of the time insisted on the submissive nature of women and her vocation of a home-maker, they were growing aware of the increasing discrepancy between their views and the contemporary reality. At the same time they began to perceive a certain thinness in their own arguments: carrying them to their logical conclusion would mean embracing one of the extreme standpoints - woman's total emancipation or her complete subjection to man. As it appears, few writers were willing to champion either radical solution. The traditional model was incompatible with the already established industrial order of society; the progressive met with little enthusiasm in the general public which found it offensive to common sense, feminine sensibility and social order. Caught in the dilemma, most writers oscillate between the extremes in an ineffectual attempt to keep the middle ground.

In this context "Our Second Girl," a short story by Harriet Beecher Stowe published in The Atlantic as early as 1868, offers an interesting argument. The newly hired, perfect servant proves at the end to be a lady of temporarily reduced means who finds it more congenial to do housework for strangers for regular hours and regular wages than for the next of kin for no pay at all. Stowe's point is directed against a false notion of gentility which prevented many a girl from taking a similar step toward independence. Stowe regards honest work for self-support preferable and more dignified than idle dependence inforced by false pride; nevertheless her general view on woman's role in society is basically traditional. Extremely active, a prolific, popular writer, she set a personal example of combining a professional career with an exemplary fulfillment of domestic duties. Nor was she the only one to achieve the successful balance between her varied interests. A number of middle class women of her talent and energy felt equal to the demands of both callings. It is significant that asking admission to education and professional recognition in a quiet, lady-like manner, they all accepted and enacted their principal social role of wives and mothers unchanged. In other words, they extended the range of their activities without attempting to reform the underlying concepts and principles. Hence, their novels hardly ever reflect advancements in woman's emancipation; paging through literary magazines, one comes occasionally across short stories which point to ridiculous or harmful effects of such new "progressive" ideas.[61]

One of them, "The Fate of the Voice" deserves
more attention because Mary Hallock Foote contrasts
two attitudes toward artistic talent, ambition and
career. Gifted with a beautiful voice, Madeline
thinks herself destined to be an artist, an opera
singer. To fulfill her vocation she is ready to
renounce love and marriage.

> A voice is a vocation in itself . . .
> My life is pledged to a purpose as
> serious as marriage itself . . .
> Love is not the only inspiration a
> woman's life can know . . . it is
> insanity of selfishness . . . [to]
> want to absorb into your life a
> thing that was meant . . . for all
> the world to share and enjoy.

Pleading his love, Aldis outlines the prospects of an
alternative career.

> . . . to a generous woman who belives
> in the regenerating influence of her
> art, I should think there would be
> a singular pleasure in giving it away
> to those who are cut off all from
> all such joys. . . . Oh, how blind
> you are to a career so much finer, so
> much broader, so much sweeter, and
> more womanly! . . . You are to sing
> to the wandering, godless peoples . . .
> of the Far West. You would have to
> give up a good deal. . . . But is
> there any virtue in woman that becomes
> her better?[62]

Like many high-minded girls Madeline does not know her
heart. A powerful shock reveals to her the potential
destructiveness of her ambition. Convinced by her
newly discovered love more than by rational arguments
she gives up her plans to become Aldis' wife: her
voice will serve higher purposes than personal vanity
or public entertainment. It will improve, educate,
and refine the rough, tense, preoccupied, man and his
business-dominated world. Her mission will be to
exercise her irresistible feminine, i.e., civilizing
influence.

The prevailing negative attitude toward the
feminists can be traced to several factors. While

124

quite willing to recognize genuine talent - a fair
number of women-writers enjoyed the esteem of their
male colleagues and readers - the majority among men
novelists considered feminist militancy as being
ridiculous and falsely grounded. Man and woman are
not natural enemies, they argued, no more, to use the
familiar phrase of the time, than the capitalist and
the worker.[63] The urge of self-assertion, reflecting
the more general disintegration of social patterns and
organization, mislead many a restless girl to aggressiveness, hence to unpleasant and unwomanly behavior.
Popular fiction distinguished clearly between feminism
and womanliness; one was incompatible with the other
and true women instinctively avoided misbehavior, even
when they wished for a larger field of activity and
freedom. In "Azalia," a short story by Joel Chandler
Harris, independent and somewhat unconventional Helen
Eustis whose "ideas were womanly rather than
feminine . . . [and] views of life in general, and of
mankind in particular, were orderly and rational"
voices the most frequent objection against the
feminist movement.

> I wouldn't give one grain of your
> common sense for all that Elizabeth
> Mappis has written or spoken. . . .
> She acts like a man in disguise.
> When I see her striding about
> delivering her harangues, I always
> imagine she is wearing a pair of
> cow-hide boots as a sort of stimulus
> to her masculinity.[64]

Such arguments imply that however capable of undertaking the same tasks as men, women, and society at
large, would lose rather than gain by introducing
a comparable uniformity. The world would be
deprived of much beauty, refinement and tenderness
so long embodied and cultivated by women sheltered at
home. The novelists seem oblivious of the fact that
under industrial conditions marriage ceased to be an
economic necessity, nor were children a highly
advantageous acquisition. The number of unmarried
women was increasing steadily, hence their social and
legal status had to be defined on new principles.
Generally speaking most novelists willingly approved
of such requests which seemed compatible with the
traditional social roles. Thus, they acknowledged the
initial goals of the women's movement, set as early
as the 1840s, which included the legal personality of

married women, freedom of person and property and access
to liberal higher education.[65] The radical demands
for political and economic equality met little favor.
Ironically, popular novels illustrating endless
sufferings of women married to worthless and heart-
less scoundrels contributed their share to the cause
of moderate emancipation.

Amidst various efforts to adjust to new conditions
most novelists subscribed to the conviction that "the
use of a truly amiable woman is to make some honest
man happy."[66] Her position, while equal to man's,
ought to be considered diametrically different, her
talents no less numerous and valuable, her duties
requiring the same degree of fortitude and intelligence.
Nevertheless, her natural sphere is personal and
private. Stepping upon a public scene she inevitably
strains her gifts beyond the point of grace and abuses
her very nature. Henry James makes ample use of
the above and many other arguments in The Bostonians
(1886), the novel dealing directly with the problem of
emancipation.

Southern conservatism renders Basil Ransom immune
to feminist accusations and reasoning: he abhors the
idea on personal as well as public ground. Attracted
by Verona's beauty he sincerely believes she is made
for love and marriage, for the ordinary joys and
troubles of domestic life. His ardent pursuit of
the girl is urged by love and the masculine desire to
win her. Carrying Verona away he asserts male
dominance, although perhaps momentarily and on a
small scale only. In doing so he is glad to checkmate
the pernicious influence of the feminist agitation
which ruins the contemporary society.

> The whole generation is womanized; the
> masculine tone is passing out of the
> world; it's a feminine, a nervous,
> hysterical, chattering, canting age,
> an age of hollow phrases and false
> delicacy and exaggerated solicitudes
> and coddled sensibilities, which, . . .
> will usher in the reign of mediocrity,
> of the feeblest and flattest and the
> most pretentious that has ever been.[67]

Ransom's attitude toward the reform movement is
altogether too contemptuous to allow personal engagement in the controversy, yet the harm done by Verona's

126

desertion contains for him, most probably, some
additional satisfaction. From his point of view,
the existing social order, imperfect as it is,
provides an adequate frame for natural needs and
desires of both sexes, while Olive's vague project
includes no such provisions.

Olive Chancellor "takes things hard," there is
something almost perverse in her excessive morbidity
which bans all thought of love, gaiety, and relax-
ation. In Ransom's words Olive is a "new spinster",
one incapable of making an honest man happy. As
far as it can be construed, her reformed world is
one of cold, bitter, restless and resentful old
maids who can offer but little comfort, cheer or
pleasure to the male half of mankind. In the early
stages of their association, Olive's only reproach is
that Verona does not detest and hate men; her greatest
fear which at one point leads her to demand a solemn
pledge of permanent virginity, is of Verona's possible
betrayal. Underestimating all natural impulses, she
deems it possible to keep Verona exclusively for
herself. Presenting the unscrupulous struggle to
possess the girl James offers no excuses for Ransom's
egotism; however, he finds his wish to win and govern
Verona more palatable than Olive's domineering
character, with her high-strung reforming zeal, and
morbid rigidity.

The few novelists who touched upon the problem of
emancipation skirted any direct confrontation. Their
usual policy was to demonstrate that anger, vehemence,
and aggressiveness, so unbecoming in a woman, were in
fact unnecessary. Every woman, they argued, commands
inexhaustible resources of wit, persuasion, and
influence which prove far more effective than feminist
campaigns and conventions.

> The best and ablest pleaders for feminine
> rights are they who, keeping their rights
> out of sight, demand and get much more
> in the name of courtesy. Men incline
> to assert themselves and prate of their
> prerogatives; but they are easily
> managed. . . . A dozen fine magnetic
> women can accomplish more . . . than a
> hundred conventions . . . All this is
> unjust, but nevertheless it is a fact,
> a firm evidence that the strength of
> woman's position must rest as a basis

on masculine weakness.[68]

To accomplish this much woman does not need to bother about her rights. She can exercise a powerful and profound influence on her surroundings by the subtle pressure of her personality. Her womanly charm will gain her more privileges and concessions than any legislative act could grant her.

Another factor contributing to the negative attitude to the women's movement was more subtle and therefore less consciously realized. The very intensity of feelings indicates that the problem was something of a threat. Significantly enough, the key argument among the conservatives was that of social order.

> Woman holds the key of social order in
> her hand . . .; to wrench it from her
> by force, to steal it from her by flattery
> would be to open the door to general
> pillage.[69]

Women's emancipation was too complex a problem to be solved by legislation or journalistic campaigns. It involved a profound change in all areas of social life; in men-women relations, their social roles, established patterns of behavior, the recognized value system. By the 1880s, the process was no longer a vague possibility but an immediate and overwhelming actuality. It spelled the final desintegration of the existing social order already disrupted by industrialization.

The task facing the intellectual elite of the country seemed obvious enough - to vindicate moral and social principles which were the foundation of the present structure of society. The long established novelistic convention of virtue rewarded by a happy marriage offered many writers of the day the ready-made frame within which they could expose folly, criticize improper or misguided conduct as well as promote the correct behavioral patterns. Character-istically, they all associate fine taste with morality: beauty and refinement are never confined to a single aspect, they permeate the entire personality of fictional characters. In the realm of fiction the ideal is embodied primarily in women capable of imposing harmony, art and virtue on modern chaotic and vulgar existence. In his study of the late

nineteenth century romances Kelly Edward Griffith
ascribes the uniformity of popular formulas used in
these novels to the underlying ideology shared by the
writers:

> . . . those with "good blood" were the
> repository for all good things, whether
> ethical, aesthetic, or political . . .
> and tried through "culture" to imbue
> the world . . . with the ideal.[70]

The preoccupation with the ideal explains, at least
partly, a certain reluctance or cautiousness in dealing
with current controversial issues which clearly yield
in importance to the central educational purpose of
fiction. Avoiding radical opinions the novelists tend
to support more workable, sensible solutions which,
accommodating the demands of the new order of things,
endorsed the basic values of the old.

The most evident compromise was reached in
redefining the concept of success. With regard to
ladies its meaning was gradually extended beyond
mere participation or leadership in society gatherings
or entertainments. True social success involved the
realization of higher aims of love, family, art, and
intellect. For women, as for men, the key to
success lies in character. The heroine must embrace
first of all the principle Christian virtues of
kindness, self-control, charity and compassion,
patience, and endurance, Thus fortified, she will
fulfill conscienciously and willingly her obligations
as a citizen contributing to maintain order, educating,
setting the right example, helping the less fortunate.
Her duties, performed most naturally and most
effectively in the family circle, require, one should
not forget, as much courage and clarity of perception
as honest business, but her moral fibre is neither
dominating nor commanding. Instead, it seeks to
influence, induce, guide and support. Her true mission
is to be a lady

> . . . full of natural refinement and
> grace, and beauty. . . She polishes them
> [men] unconsciously . . . using her
> gentle influence to lift and hold them above
> the coarse, rough things of life and keep
> them gentlemen in the best sense of the
> fine old word.[74]

Ideal woman was to embody those qualities and accomplishments which would make the world better, a more wholesome and humane place to live.

In projecting this ideal the novelists of the time meet their own obligation as writers - that literature should aim beyond mere entertainment or even beauty. Its proper function is to disseminate ideas, to teach and uplift their audience. However, all such efforts to ingrain the traditional values and illustrate them in popular novels bear witness to the increasing awareness that old norms and virtues were losing their relevance in the rapidly changing industrial and urban conditions. The novelists found it impossible to remain neutral or to elude confrontation with new social issues; the very insistence on the didactic massage forestalls the near future when, for better or worse, economic, social and intellectual forces operating in America would definitely sweep old models away.

Notes

1. In the preceding discussion on business and
   success, the term society referred to American
   population at large, regardless of wealth, class
   or professional affiliation. Here the word will
   be used primarily in its narrower meaning, denoting
   a comparatively small section of the affluent
   leisure class whose wealth allows entertainment
   while society life as well as diverse artistic
   pursuits become primary occupations. "Culture"
   should be understood broadly as covering
   behavioral patterns and precepts controlling
   social roles and intercourse. It includes norms
   and values which more or less consciously motivate
   human actions and choices. The "high" or
   intellectual and artistic aspects are regarded of
   secondary importance to the present considerations.

2. J. L. Allen, "The White Cowl," The Century,
   September 1888, p. 691.

3. G. A. Hibbard, "The Woman in the Case," The Century,
   June 1889, p. 213. The theme is of primary
   importance in such novels as F. H. Burnett,
   Through One Administration, E. P. Roe, Without
   a Home, and Francis Lynde, The Helpers, but it
   appears in many others as well.

4. Abigail Roe, Free, Yet Forging Their Own Chains
   (New York, 1876), p. 301. Cf. J. G. Holland,
   Sevenoaks (New York, 1875), pp. 208-10; E. O. Kirk,
   Queen Money (Boston, 1889), pp. 299-300.

5. Etiquette books frequently insist that true
   gentility begins with paying unreserved respect
   to all women regardless of their social status.
   Cf.: "It has been wisely remarked that the true
   advancement of a nation may be exactly determined
   by the position of its women. According as
   mothers of the race are respected and cherished
   will the sons be wise, noble and unselfish."
   E. B. Duffey, The Ladies' and Gentlemen's
   Etiquette (Philadelphia, 1877), p. 12.

6. H. C. Christy, The American Girl as Seen and
   Presented by . . . (New York, 1906), pp. 25, 108.

7. Jean Webster, Daddy-Long-Legs (New York, 1912).

8. E. O. Kirk, p. 103.

9. Cf. A. M. Douglas, Hope Mills (Boston, 1879),
    p. 301. Sylvie "will always spur a man up to his
    best. Her well-trained ear is quick to detect
    a false note in honor, ambition, or love. She
    will never be any kind of dead weight, and yet
    she is so deliciously womanly." Also Kirk, p.
    483. Lucy is preaching: "Otto, I want you to
    be just as good and brave and self-denying and
    pure as a man can be. I want you to begin this
    moment and put by aims and ends which are not
    the best aims and ends."

10. Henry James, "Manners of American Women" and
    "Speech of American Women," in French Writers
    and American Women Essays, (Bradford, Conn.,
    1960).

11. Albert Rhodes, "The Marriage Question," Galaxy,
    December 1875, p. 764. Cf. Fuller, The Cliff-
    Dwellers (New York, 1893), pp. 249-51.

12. "It is . . . the duty of every woman to make
    herself as beautiful as possible; nor is it less
    the duty of every man to render himself pleasing
    in appearance. . . . We owe it to ourselves
    because others estimate us very naturally and
    very rightly by our outward appearance, and we
    owe it to others because we have no right to put
    our friends to the blush by untidiness or
    uncouthness." Duffey, p. 225.

13. J. C. Dorr, Bride and Bridegroom (Cincinnati,
    1873), p. 199.

14. H. W. Papashvily, All the Happy Endings (New York,
    1956), p. 20.

15. J. C. Dorr, p. 139.

16. Cf. Ann Douglas, The Feminization of American
    Culture (New York, 1977), pp. 48-49. H. W.
    Papashvily presents similar arguments though
    she does not use the term.

17. C. F. Pierce, "Co-Operative Housekeeping,"
    The Atlantic, November 1868, p. 518.

18. Rhodes, p. 728.

19. J. H. Browne, "Women's Rights Aesthetically," _Galaxy_, May 1871, p. 725.

20. _Ibid_., p. 727.

21. O. W. Holmes, "The Americanized Europe," _The Atlantic_, January 1875, p. 85.

22. Rhodes, p. 763.

23. After a prolonged European stay James found the results of his polarization appalling. "That truth is simply that the women, on our side of the world, actually enjoy and use authority, pleading in no other connection whatever the least unfitness for it. They have taken it over without blinking, they are encamped on every inch of the social area that the stock exchange and the baseball field leave free; the whole social initiative is in other words theirs, having been abandoned to them without struggle." "The Speech of American Women" in _French Writers_ . . . , p. 39.

24. John DeForest, _Honest John Vane_, _The Atlantic_, July 1873, p. 68.

25. Pierce, p. 519.

26. F. H. Hall, _Social Customs_ (Boston, 1887), p. 268.

27. John DeForest, _Honest John Vane_, R. H. Davis, _John Andross_.

28. For variant I see: Julie D. Whitling, "The Story of Myra," _The Century_, July 1884; Rose Terry Cooke, "Too Late," _Galaxy_, January 1875; for variant II: Joseph Kirkland, _Zury: the Meanest Man in Spring County_ (Boston, 1887).

29. John Hay, _The Breadwinners_ (New York, 1884), p. 41.

30. Kate Chopin, _The Awakening_ (New York, 1964), p. 47.

31. _Ibid_., p. 33.

32. R. Gordon Kelly, _Mother Was a Lady_ (Westport, Conn., 1974), p. 43.

33. Ella Williams, "Mrs. Job Grey," _Galaxy_, May 1871, p. 723.

34. Hall, pp. 100-101.

35. M. E. W. Sherwood, _The Art of Entertaining_ (New York, 1892), p. 385.

36. Edith Wharton, _The Age of Innocence_ (New York, 1920), p. 100.

37. Fuller, p. 228.

38. Kirk, p. 248.

39. C. D. Warner, _A Little Journey in the World_ (Ridgewood, N.J., 1967), p. 355.

40. Ibid., p. 383.

41. R. H. Davis, _John Andross_ (New York, 1874), p. 241.

42. Everett Carter, _Howells and The Age of Realism_ (Hamden, Conn., 1966), pp. 38-39.

43. Howells, _The Rise of Silas Lapham_ (New York, 1958), p. 180.

44. Stow Persons, _The Decline of American Gentility_ (New York, 1973), p. 93.

45. Ibid., p. 120.

46. Henry James, Sr., "The Woman Thou Gavest With Me," _The Atlantic_, January 1870, pp. 68-69.

47. Washington Gladden, "The Increase of Divorce," _The Century_, January 1882, p. 415.

48. Ibid., p. 418.

49. Howells, _A Modern Instance_ (New York, 1964), p. 387.

50. Ibid., p. 200.

51. Henry James, <u>The Golden Bowl</u> (New York, 1963), p. 426.

52. <u>Ibid</u>., p. 425.

53. Dorothea Krook, <u>The Ordeal of Consciousness in Henry James</u> (Cambridge, Mass., 1962), p. 278.

54. Wharton, <u>The Age of Innocence</u>, p. 42.

55. <u>Ibid</u>., p. 350.

56. <u>Ibid</u>., p. 352.

57. Robert Grant, <u>An Average Man</u>, <u>The Century</u>, December 1883 - July 1884, May 1884, p. 92. Cf. George Hibbard, "Induna," <u>The Century</u>, May 1886. The short story illustrates the fatal consequences of hiding the truth. Isolated from the outside world, Induna grows ignorant of the existence of death. The inevitable shattering experience of her older sister's death incapacitates her for love and happiness. Becoming a nun she seeks immortality in religion.

58. Grant, May 1884, p. 93.

59. Cf. Rhodes, p. 764: "The woman is not advised to go out of her domestic sphere and pursue the callings of men except so far as it may be necessary for her material welfare and intellectual serenity. That organization is best which permits the wife and daughter to perform their duties at home in the bosom of the family. For this reason such callings should be selected as will admit of being pursued in the home circle." Rhodes' suggestions, discussed in detail in "Women's Occupations," <u>Galaxy</u>, January 1876, include painting, literature, drawing, wood engraving, making of artificial flowers, bonnet and dress making. Characteristically, they are all "womanly occupations". Also: G. Andrews, "Make Your Daughter Independent," <u>The Century</u>, Open Letters, May 1888.

60. E. L. Holman, "Another Side to the Woman's Work Question," <u>The Century</u>, Open Letters, May 1888, p. 317. Cf. J. H. Browne, "Woman's

Rights Aesthetically."

61. Cf. M. A. Edwards, "Pamela Clerke," Galaxy,
     September 1866, "Progressive Baby," Galaxy,
     May 1877, M. L. Bradley, "Helen," The Century,
     October, 1887.

62. M. H. Foote, "The Fate of a Voice," The Century,
     November 1886, p. 63.

63. Cf. Rhodes, p. 758: "Among these self-appointed
     leaders are the turbulent women who endeavor to
     advance interests of their sex by reviling men as
     their one particular enemy. . . . when man is in
     question they are often vituperative . . . the
     fighting is all on one side. The hen may peck
     the male bird but he does not return it."

64. J. C. Harris, "Azalia," The Century, August 1887,
     p. 550.

65. Mt. Holyoke Seminary, the first to offer higher
     education to women in 1837, was followed by
     Elmira College in 1855, Vasser 1865, Wellesley
     Seminary 1870, Smith College 1871, Bryn Mawr
     1880, Radcliffe 1879. The earliest legislation
     included the right to hold property in New York,
     1848, voting rights in Wyoming Territory, 1889,
     10 hours work day in Massachusetts, 1874,
     prohibition of employment in mining in Illinois,
     1879.

66. Henry James, The Bostonians (Penguin 1971),
     p. 206.

67. Ibid., p. 290.

68. Browne, p. 729.

69. Morgan Dix, Lectures on the Calling of a
     Christian Woman (New York, 1883), p. 13.

70. K. E. Griffith, The Genteel Romance in American
     Literature 1880-1910. Unpublished Ph.D.
     dissertation, University of Pennsylvania 1968,
     p. 210.

71. L. M. Alcott, Little Men (New York, 1962), p. 313.

Part Three

THE NOVELIST

In his essay of 1913 "Genteel Tradition in
American Philosophy" George Santayana took for his
point of departure the profound split in American
consciousness - one separating the practical sphere
of life from intellectual pursuits and endeavors.

> The division may be found symbolized
> in American architecture; a neat
> reproduction of the colonial mansion -
> with some modern comforts introduced
> surreptitiously - stands beside the
> sky-scraper. The American Will
> inhabits the sky-scraper; the American
> Intellect inhabits the colonial
> mansion. The one sphere is of the
> American man; the other, at least
> predominantly, of the American
> Woman. The one is all aggressive
> enterprise; the other is all genteel
> tradition.[1]

This divergence between the practical and
intellectual sphere is one more illustration of the
polarization of American activity into the world
of men and the world of women discussed in the
preceding sections. The first and foremost of
numerous consequences of this division was the
dominant influence of women, their tastes and
sensibilities, on the general tone of American
thought, arts, and literature. The notion underlies
most writing on the subject, so that to say that
in the second half of the nineteenth century the
American reading public was composed predominantly,
if not exclusively, of women has all the qualifications
of a cliche. Hjorth Hjalmar Boyesen's once
extremely influential essay "Why We Have No Great
Novelists" (1887) argued that this female audience
imposed a highly restrictive censorship upon American
writers which, suppressing passions, trimming the
language, watering down ideas, and stifling every
serious thought, hampered the development of the
native literature. Boyesen's vision of "the Iron
Madonna who strangles in her fond embrace the American
Novelist"[2] may well have been exaggerated, though,
on the other hand, Mark Twain's well-known, and most

willing, submission to the "grooming" of his wife and daughters seems to confirm Boyesen's bitter accusations.

The actual situation was probably more complex. There is enough sound evidence that literary magazines were read by men as well as women, the "Open Letters" department in The Century being the most reliable and interesting source of information. The considerable number of serious articles on current economic, social and philosophical topics seems to indicate that the editors catered to the tastes and interests of both sexes in equal measure. William Dean Howells, editor of literary magazines for more than twenty years (first of The Atlantic 1866-1881, then of Harper's 1886-1891), knew his audience at first hand; his letters as well as "Editor's Study" in Harper's indicate his familiarity with both his male and female readers. At the same time he seems less apprehensive of their limitations and the neces- sity to court their favor. And yet he must have had valid reasons for outlining the role of women in promoting arts as he did in A Hazard of New Fortunes.

> We've got to recognize that women
> form three fourth of the reading
> public in this country, and go for
> their tastes and their sensibilities
> and their sex-piety along the whole
> line. They do like to think that
> women can do things better than men;
> and if we can let it leak out . . .
> that . . . Every Other Week couldn't
> stir a peg . . . till they got a lot
> of God-gifted girls to help them, it'll
> make the fortune of the thing.[3]

Howells' authority should not be disregarded: he clearly considered intelligent country women the most serious and appreciating readers who could, and did, decide a novel's success or failure.[4] However, his opinion may well reflect a more general con- viction that in all matters pertaining to culture the final word belonged to women.

Under such circumstances, the position of a novelist was hardly enviable, even if the require- ments and restrictions imposed upon his art were less deadly than those of Boyesen's Iron Madonna. In the highly polarized society a male writer was

often placed socially in an uncomfortable "in-between"
position. By sex he belonged to the enterprising,
competitive, acquisitive world of men and business in
which intellectual pursuits and literary interests
enjoyed little prestige. Writing was hardly a
masculine occupation; with other cultural endeavors
it had been ceded to and claimed by women. Since it
demanded neither physical exertion nor technical skill
nor financial shrewdness, tough self-made business
men were inclined to class writers together with
clergymen. Both seemed to belong to a separate
species of slightly feminized character. It seems
particularly significant that etiquette books of the
period, so competent in settling the most intricate
social problems, draw attention to the undefined
position of artists, musicians, and writers. Gerald
Garson quotes one writer who "commented with sympathy
that these professional people were apt to be hyper-
sensitive, since they do not know precisely where they
stand."[5] "Scribbling - women" faced no such dilemma
because their social position was defined without
qualifications by sex. The merger of the two groups,
women and men of letters, could never be complete,
though their alliance produced many specific
characteristics of American culture.[6]

Professionally, many writers were connected
either with journalism or editing or publishing, at
least in the early stages of their careers. Howells
and Holland worked as editors, Mark Twain served for
a while as a reporter. Those who did not hold
permanent jobs usually secured regular income by
signing a contract with one of the literary or
popular magazines for a fixed number of contributions
over a certain period of time, usually a year. Hamlin
Garland made use of the practices at one point, as
did James, Howells, R. H. Davis and good many
others. In the final decades of the century magazines
clearly dominate the literary scene for at least two
reasons. They provided in a single volume reading
material of high quality and great variety: biographies,
literary or historical essays, political and economic
debates, travel sketches, short stories, poems, and
novels. They enabled even the remotest country towns
and farms to "keep up" with new currents of thought
and the literary tastes of the Eastern seaboard
elite. Secondly, until the International Copyright
Law of 1891, magazine serial publications offered
American writers practically the only chance of
reaching the public and gaining recognition. The

139

book market was flooded with extremely cheap editions of excellent foreign novels in comparison with which native literature, for which royalties had to be paid, proved a far less lucrative business to the publisher.

To the entire generation reaching maturity during and shortly after the Civil War, the New England sages - Oliver Wendell Holmes, Henry Wadsworth Longfellow, R. W. Emerson, J. G. Whittier, James Russell Lowell - embodied the highest achievement of American letters. Generally admired and respected, their work set standards of quality for readers, as well as for many a young apprentice venturing into literature. The high prestige they enjoyed expressed more than the affinity of taste and thought between Boston Brahmins and their audience. The dominant characteristics of their work - traditional patterns, language, poetic diction, ideas expressed - was transferred from an earlier era and spanned over the war experience to produce a sense of continuity with the past. They infused classical order of thought and poetic expression into the post-war confusion deepened by the turmoil of industrialization. Thus, they responded to the profound wish for unity in the temporal as well as spatial dimension. The New England sages were actually best qualified to affirm and voice an unbroken literary and intellectual tradition. However, this very effort to maintain the continuity incapacitated them from incorporating the currents and forces re-shaping the American reality of the 1870s in artistic form. Also, New England, or more precisely Boston, which dominated their perspective, offered too narrow a frame of reference to embrace the entire continent in all its diversity.[7] This crucial task was to be achieved by writers of the next generation born between 1835-1845 (quite a few of them west of the Alleghanies). Therefore, the first visit of young William Dean Howells to Boston in 1860, to pay his reverent respects to Lowell, was charged with almost symbolic significance; Holmes called it, half humorously, "the apostolic succession . . . the laying on of hands."

> What was being passed on was the
> quiet power of neo-classical Brahmin
> culture, flowing from its restricted
> core of Boston into the whole of
> American life, and somehow, Holmes
> sensed that this small young man
> from Ohio was going to be the medium

through which that power was transmitted.[8]

Howells' allegiance to the "Brahmin culture" was rooted
in his whole-hearted adherence to the basic concept of
human existence as permeated with a profound moral
significance. His formal education was perhaps less
thorough than Henry Adams'; nevertheless the two men
shared a very similar vision of life. Looking backward in 1900 Henry Adams commented:

> Viewed from Mt. Vernon Street the
> problem of life was as simple as it
> was classic. Politics offered no
> difficulties for there the moral law
> was the surest guide. Social
> perfection was also sure, because human
> nature worked for the Good, and three
> instruments were all she asked - Suffrage,
> Common Schools, and Press. On these
> points doubt was forbidden, Education
> was divine, and man needed only a correct
> knowledge of facts to reach perfection.[9]

This vision of a rational and moral universe, in
which every human being is capable of advancement and
perfection if only he gains access to an understanding
of the facts, stands behind all Howells' writing. As
a critic and a novelist he strove to fuse the old
values into contemporary American life; or rather, he
sought to reveal them beneath the ruthless, grasping
and materialistic industrial capitalism of his days.
As the editor of The Atlantic, the principal forum of
Brahmin culture ever since its founding in 1857,
Howells availed himself of the power and influence
of his position to promote the new school of realism.
True to the actual, exploring common events and
experiences of ordinary people, realistic fiction
presented facts and brought to the surface their
meaning, pattern and value. Howells was evidently
sharing tacitly Basil March's final comment "I believe
it means good."[10]

By nineteenth century standards Howells' career
was definitely a success. The editorship of The
Atlantic opened numerous advantages, among which
financial security and public influence did not
count the least. He found Boston atmosphere congenial
and soon made himself at home there: he subscribed
to its code of gentlemanly respectability out of
temperament as well as from conscious choice.

141

A recognized heir to New England sages, a successor
to their authority, he worked his opportunities to
the full. He lead the struggle for realism and
against sentimentalism, encouraged, advised, and
published many of his innovative contemporaries and
promising younger authors - the efforts which gained
him the unique title of the Dean of American letters
in later years. It seemed only fair and natural that
his writing profession proved highly renumerative.
Everet Carter quotes that "by 1885 Howells was the
highest paid American novelist, reportedly able to
demand five thousand dollars for a serial, besides
a royalty on the published book."[11]

Few of his contemporaries were as lucky or
privileged. As professional writers they all faced
the problem of securing a decent and steady income.
To capture the curiosity and to meet the expectations
of their readers they resorted to popular concepts,
already successful formulas, well-known topics and
sentiments. Horatio Alger was by no means the only
one to rewrite his one story in so many versions.
Elizabeth Stuart Phelps used the initial idea of
The Gates Ajar (1868) to win top sales in 1883
with Beyond the Gates and again in 1887 with The Gates
Between. Western humor, local color tales, romances
of Christian virtue and piety, domestic novels were
but few of many types of popular fiction which could
command a steady and fairly wide, profit-making market.
Popular fiction included books as different as Mark
Twain's Roughing It and E. P. Roe's Barriers Burned
Away, both published in 1872. The artistic quality of
bestsellers varied as much, but the fact did not
actually affect their immediate sales. Such courting
of popular taste and prevailing sentiments seems
natural enough. It is far more significant that few
popular novelists, who admittedly secured favorable
reception by reproducing stock characters and plots,
considered themselves merely entertainers. Popular
novels of the period could appeal to pious sentiments
or the desire for the sensational: in either case
they are marked by the same didactic strain. Moral
laws are never questioned: wickedness meets well-
deserved punishment while virtue reaps its just
reward. The long established convention is usually
further amplified by some additional message of
social or spiritual importance.

Amidst turbulent social transformations most
writers appear to believe sincerely that their novels

could and should educate while entertaining. Hence
their efforts to combine both elements - to meet the
demands of their conscience while ensuring a satis-
factory income - may be considered as devoid of hypocrisy. Both goals of financial gain and didactic
message were worthy of pursuing, the double motivation,
openly admitted, seemed no less honest for being
double. What the novelists failed to realize perhaps,
was that this joint purpose was, in fact, an
unconscious response to their ill-defined social
status. The financial part was first of all dictated
by necessity, yet, if profits happened to be
spectacular, or at least handsome, they affirmed the
author's participation in the competitive, money-
earning business community. His self-appointed role
as teacher and censor of contemporary society carried
a far greater weight. Assuming the duties and
responsibilities of an educator, the novelist created
for himself a separate "social space," a specific
area of social action "in between" the polarized
extremes of business and "society." Hence, his
efforts were consistently directed to expose evil,
correct abuses and follies, promote socially desirable
social behavior, disseminate new ideas, and inculcate
an optimistic faith in an orderly, rational, and moral
universe. Presenting possible unity or fusion between
the two groups, he sought to bridge the disturbing
split in American society.

     Since the two spheres seemed diametrically
opposed, the differences being strongly emphasized,
the novelists' delicate task was to counteract numerous
preconceived and falsely grounded notions. Outlining
their characters they take care to dissociate manliness from mere physical force and the simplicity of
an uncultivated mind. A usual hero type possessed
all the best features of masculine beauty, the
impressions of which are always accompanied by
corresponding qualities of character. His bodily
strength indicates firm will, just as the open,
cheerful countenance tells of his frank and genial
disposition. Yet neither handsome looks nor manual
skills nor even business shrewdness avail him much if
his spiritual faculties remain uncultivated. The
gradual development of natural qualities appears a
frequent theme in the novels of the period, sometimes
as far apart in their artistic merits as Howells'
The Landlord at Lion's Head (1897) and E. P. Roe's
Without a Home (1881). The latter novel takes the
sentimental view of an uncouth country boy who wakes

143

up to the possibility of better and higher life when stirred by love for a beautiful, accomplished upper middle class girl whom he marries, of course, at the end of the story.

If a popular hero happens to be a "flat" character, the tale of his fortune is "round"; the narrators keep careful balance between his material and cultural advancement. Incidents of the plot are generally arranged to reveal both sides of his personality alternately so that they may convince the reader that social refinement is fully compatible with business success. The hero is no less manly for being well-mannered and appreciative of art; his personal grace and ease in society gatherings go hand in hand with his ability to control an unruly mob of strikers, defy a dishonest speculator, or meet as dire an emergency as the Chicago fire of 1871 or a flood. True manliness need not involve boorishness or ignorance; nor are cultivated taste and intellectual interests signs of a weakened, effeminate nature.

A similar attitude prevails with reference to the heroine. Usually beautiful, or at least extremely good-looking, she is modelled according to the ideal of perfect womanhood. Her "delicacy of feeling, educated refinement of mind not always found among the belles of elite society,"[12] however, are seldom associated with weakness or superficiality. Her tender, soft, often yielding disposition screens firmness and force of character. Whenever circumstances demand it, she displays an amazing capacity for quick judgment and prompt action guided by courage and common sense; characteristically, she appears no less womanly or ladylike under the strain. Her feminine grace is enhanced by the rule of reason and clear purpose in life.

In the usual "boy-meets-girl" plot in which both characters embody the ideal of their respective sexes, their marriage signifies more than a happy end to youthful adventure. Their union brings the opposites together. The hero's social grace and well trained artistic perception blends harmoniously with the heroine's natural sensitivity to beauty, as expressed on the one hand in her accomplishments in music, painting, or literature, and on the other in her skill for producing aesthetic effects in daily housekeeping. At the same time, the wide range of her intellectual and public interests, her keen

insight and sound judgment enable her husband to
share with her his professional cares and ambitions,
his hopes, plans, and difficulties; she is capable
of understanding, sympathizing, and advising. With
such advantages, their marriage - a genuine union of
souls - should ensure peace, stability and happiness
for both.

This message is conveyed primarily through the
turns of fictional events designed to draw the
reader's attention to complementary qualities of
character and accomplishments of the hero and the
heroine. The novelists avail themselves of negative
evidence as frequently, i.e. they emphasize those
features of the "third party's" character which
disqualify him or her from marrying the heroine,
or the hero. To give but one example: in Queen Money
(1889) Ellen O. Kirk describes Barry Charnock courting
the heroine, Lucy Florian. His declaration of love
comes only in the middle of the story after the reader
has observed him in various situations. The very fact
that he postpones his declaration until he accumulates
enough money counts against him. Paying regular
visits at Lucy's home, he lets her friends and
acquaintances assume their engagement is as good as
announced - though he never asked the girl's consent.
Noticing her interest in her cousin, Otto, and fearing
his personal attractiveness, he is mean enough to
appeal to Otto's magnaminity by claiming priority to
Lucy's affections. He knows his rival is too honorable
not to withdraw his attentions, no matter what he
feels. Finally, E. O. Kirk indicates other deficiencies of his character: he is eager to gain money
without inquiring too closely into the moral nature
of the deal, as long as the transaction is safe and
profitable. He lacks courage and stamina to endure
risks and suspense calmly; he also lacks self-control
to resist the temptation of gambling, nor can he bear
his losses in a manly way. Naturally, such attitudes
and technical tricks dominate novels built of stock
characters and ready-made formulas.

Most novelists of the period adhere to the conventional view of the roles appropriate for the sexes
and supported the traditional division of social
functions. Nevertheless, they try to minimize the
existing opposition between masculine and feminine
interests by putting more emphasis on the complementary nature of their respective characteristics,
inclinations, and duties. The power of mutual

attraction, they seem to argue, more often lies in
similarities in disposition, interests, and amusements
than in differences and contention. Consciously or
not, the novelist's conviction finds its reflection
in language. A close reading of popular novels
indicates that the very same adjectives are used in
reference to both sexes, and with comparable
frequency. Commenting on the manly bearing of his
hero, a novelist may well qualify the tone of his
voice as quiet or tender. Put to the test, confronted
with injustice or humiliation he never loses self-
control, so his actions stay resolute and decisive
but "marked by the dignity of a refined and cultivated
person." At the same time, the events of the plot
may call forth the heroine's "dormant strength and
energy." Gay and lighthearted, she can be as firm
and resolute as any businessman and yet remain sweet
in her earnestness.

These writers appear convinced that beyond outward
distinctions due to sex, human nature is essentially
the same: subjected to careful nourishment and
cultivation it achieves its finest shape - "pure,
strong and noble manhood or womanhood." Each finds
its external expression according to temperament,
abilities, social standing and education of the
individual, yet this variety of manifestations should
not obliterate the essential unity beyond apparent
diversity. This emphasis seems singular if we consider concurrent insistence of the very same authors
on the division of social roles and tasks. Their
double attitude may well reflect a half realized
desire to affirm unity; if so, it also explains their
simplified view of successful life, claiming that
regardless of sex, calling or circumstances, success
depends solely upon one's character. To meet one's
obligations as a Christian, a citizen, and a gentleman
or a lady, one must cultivate virtue, order, and self-
control.

The fundamental oneness of human nature is further
reflected in stock characters and situations copied
from one novel to another. In most novels the main
character, whether male or female, is a likeable young
person of middle class background, respectable even
if poor, as it usually happens. A certain discrepancy
in social position between the hero and the heroine
provides the plot with additional complications, but
the distance between them is created and measured by
money only. In terms of values, norms, and conventions

both actually belong to the same world. If he is a
poor youth striving to win his fortune and to make
a place for himself in the world, he falls in love,
as a rule, with a girl slightly above him in education
and social graces, as do Dennis Fleet in Barriers
Burned Away by E. P. Roe (1885), Richard Arbyght in
M. A. Foran's The Other Side (1885), or Arthur Wilson
in Denison's An Iron Crown (1885). Rich and all too
proud of their advantages and distinctions girls
like Irene Lawrence in Hope Mills by Amanda Douglas
(1879) or Christine Ludolph, the heroine of Barriers
Burned Away, they undergo a "change of heart" before
they become humbler but nobler wives of the model
success hero. Stories of a poor girl marrying
someone of superior standing in wealth, class and
education occur, at least in the chosen sample, less
frequently than in the European tradition. Among
the late nineteenth century novels discussed above
only three involve such a union: W. D. Howells' The
Lady of the Aroostook (1879), Henry Fuller's The
Cliff-Dwellers (1893) and The Portion of Labor by
M. W. Freeman (1901).

The figure of a villain has his female counterpart
in a "temptress"; both scheme to manipulate and
beguile the naive, unsuspecting innocents. He is
usually an unscrupulous speculator, she a brilliant
society woman; the two use their personal talents for
utterly selfish ends, either because they contempt-
uously reject all moral and public obligations or,
the less frequent variant, because they were never
taught to recognize them. Their energies and
ambitions are focused on success, power and influence,
yet since these goals are unworthy, they inevitably
end in failure.

The novelists seem to distinguish neatly between
a wrong course of action motivated by base or selfish
impulses and a comparably unacceptable behavior
resulting from faulty education. The first set of
circumstances produces a villain, the other, a victim.
To a certain extent, they are willing to class as a
victim the "dandy" type who, brought up in luxury by
indifferent or indulgent parents, thinks himself too
good for the commonplace task of earning a living.
He lacks nerve, skill as well as will for the manly
business competition. The parallel examples of girls
victimized by misdirected education or unsuitable
marriage have been discussed above.

147

In terms of plots and situations, popular novels offer us little variety; the "boy meets girl" tale usually constitutes the central axis of action. In a small minority of books including The Rise of Silas Lapham by Howells (1885), E. S. Phelps' The Silent Partner (1872) or Money Captain by William Payne (1893), the indispensable sentimental interest remains of secondary importance. With the only exception of Mark Twain there was hardly a writer who would risk a novel without a love ingredient inserted to enliven the plot. The adventures of Huck Finn, his Connecticut Yankee and his innocents abroad seem to prove the rule by being rare exceptions to it.

The usual love story ending, of course, in a blissful engagement is complicated by many combinations of other stereotyped plots. The three most popular present "innocence tempted and saved," the schemer (either a speculator vilain or an intriguing temptress), overreaching his/herself and falling in his/her own snares, and finally, vice and sin punished by a gradual decay - be it moral, social or physical. There exist other variants too, based on common fairy tale patterns of cinderella, sleeping beauty, and fairy god-mother, but they seem overshadowed by the American myth of self-made success and optimistic individualism.

Thus, popular novels of the closing decades of the nineteenth century display the same uniformity of employed formulas and stock characters that can be observed in the ideas they promote. The phenomenon has been interpreted in various ways. W. T. Ihamon argues that the narrowed scope of American novels and their increasing uniformity reflect the more pro-found shift from pluralism to monism in American culture. The process of rapid levelling and standardization of society affected literature as much as all other areas of American life. As American experience had been growing urban, industrial and middle class, so its literary expression bore the very same characteristics. The larger scope of viewpoints, and variety of characters, situations and problems yield to the prevailing single type of a middle class hero and the dominant middle class perspective. Ihamon ascribes this process to the devious, warping influence of Horatio Alger stories.

> Preceding Alger was a period of tremendous
> ambivalence and consequent rich

148

complexity in American literature. His
slightly older contemporaries included
Sinclair, Norris, Howells, Twain,
Wharton and James. That is, the wide
thematic diversity in the nineteenth
century included illiterate boys on
rivers, educated American girls in
Europe, Lithuanian immigrants in
Chicago, wheat growers in California
and gentility society in New York drawing
rooms. The literature reflected the
society's genuine pluralism. Alger's
novels, however, came at the time when
that pluralism began to decline toward
the seeming one-dimensionality of modern
society and modern literature.[13]

Ihamon's point, however, is too cursory to be tenable.
Born in 1834, Alger belonged to the same generation
as Mark Twain, Howells and James even though the
popularity of his books reached its highest mark
only after his death in 1899;[14] Edith Wharton, Norris
and Upton Sinclair, born 1862, 1870, 1878 respectively,
were his juniors by some thirty years. The general
tendency toward favor middle class notions and values
cannot be denied, yet with all his popularity Horatio
Alger appears too small a figure to bear the blame
for the change.[15] Like his contemporaries he was
caught in the complex network of social forces and,
responding to their pressure, sought to endow them
with meaning. As has been pointed out, he relied
largely on the models of the past; to make him
responsible for the profound change in American
culture means to grant him powers beyond his actual
status.

The explanation suggested by R. Gordon Kelly
appears more convincing, since it is definitely far
better documented. Popular novels, like children's
short stories of the same period which Kelly
analysed, are basically formulaic. He traces the
writers' adherence to ready-made patterns to more
serious causes and motives than deficiencies in
literary talent or imagination.

It seems likely that the social
functions of popular formulas, and
especially formulas for children's
literature, have their origins, in
part, in the precariousness of

149

social order and the consequent need
in any society or large social group
to reaffirm continually the structure
of meanings, the cultural knowledge,
that orders social behavior.[16]

Popular literature is addressed to a wide and
unsophisticated public. To fulfill its educational
purpose it must present an unequivocal image of the
world. Hence, to eliminate ambiguities and double
interpretations, the novelists resorted to well defined and easily recognizable figures and situations.
In the last quarter of the nineteenth century the
message still seemed more important than the purely
artistic effect.

     Most scholars dealing with the period share
the opinion that the precariousness of social
organization dominates the American experience of the
three decades after the Civil War. Genuine improvements, the scope and energy of new enterprises were
welcomed with appreciation, sometimes with
enthusiasm. But even the most beneficial and
spectacular achievements bred a sense of uneasiness
because they frequently entailed passive, almost
helpless surrender to pressures and forces too complex
and overwhelming to be individually or personally
controlled. Economically, the last quarter of the
century knew little peace or stability; Edward C.
Kirkland suggests that

               . . . the whole era between 1860 and
               1900 shook the business structure by a
               succession of tremblers. The first
               was the American Civil War . . . After
               a brief interval of respite and
               recuperation, there ensued a series of
               business panics and depressions. Two
               of them, 1873 and 1893, join 1837 and
               1929 as the worst in American history:
               that of the mid-eighties, though less
               calamitous, slowed and distorted the
               economy.[17]

Other areas of public life were affected by a
similar absence of reassurance and security. If
there was much exuberant oversimplifying and
triumphant enthusiasm for new industrial developments,
it often aimed to silence dismal predictions dictated
by sombre realities of class conflicts, urban poverty,

immigration, corruption of public and personal mores.

Amidst bewildering changes and general instability, the American middle class sought reassurance in the genteel tradition. The intense idealism with which the period is generally credited offered a steadfast, reliable balance to doubts and fears concerning the validity of the fundamental truths of American civic faith: individualism, optimism, progress, democracy and the Union. At the same time it helped to minimize the significance of the gross and ever growing materialism of the day, emphasizing the open possibility of freedom and advancement for everyone on the one hand, and on the other indicating the civilizing potential of wealth.

From the very beginning of the United States, ideology served as a unifying force or principle holding together a country which lacked any natural center or tangible unifying core.[18] Discussing the problem of assimilation in the nineteenth century, Professor John Higham of John Hopkins University draws attention to the fact that American citizenship depended solely on voluntary subscription to a set of political principles and ideological tenets which, granted the general diffusion of power, enabled immigrants to retain their ethnic and cultural identity while embracing the uniform American creed. This pre-eminence of ideas allowed the nineteenth century Americans to accept "complacently disparities between their theory and their practice."

> A capacity to entertain both of these
> sets of beliefs, applying them select-
> ively to different situations and
> avoiding any fundamental reckoning
> by all manner of equivocation, evasion,
> and compromise - that capacity to minimize,
> ignore, and defuse the contradictions was
> essential to the stability of American
> society in the nineteenth century. The
> one serious attempt to resolve an
> elemental contradiction tore the nation
> apart in 1861.[19]

The very same tendency to disregard contradictions and elude confrontations which could bring disparities too sharply to focus can be observed in American culture and social life. The same deeply rooted instinct to accommodate rather than oppose explains, at least

partially, the employer's general lip-service to the
model of moral purity while his business practices
belied any such contiguity between the ideal and the
actual. It throws also light upon tenacity of the
model of "ideal womanhood" which seemed to suffer no
loss of its persuasive power even as more and more
women entered labor market and public life. As
Professor Higham suggests, "to ease the strains inherent
in a culture of contradictions," individuals thought
and behaved "discrepantly on different levels of
experience or in different social settings." If their
lack of consistency involved hypocrisy, this hypocrisy seems strangely sincere because it remains but
dimly, if at all, aware of the double standards,
illusions, compromises, and self-deceptions it
practiced.

In the final decades of the century, the genteel
tradition still functioned as the unifying cultural
ideology, i.e. a set of norms and ideas the
acceptance of which served as a password to social
recognition. According to Howard Mumford Jones, this
"operative fusion of idealism and the instinct for
craftsmanship . . . dominated high culture from 1865
to 1915."

> Its idealism was at once moral,
> aesthetic, and philosophical . . .
> If idealism was the tenor, culture
> was usually the vehicle of their
> crusade. . . . Hence, the endless
> concern . . . not merely for the ideal,
> but for the ideal form, for the
> doctrine that the highest morality
> requires the most perfect expression.[20]

The very effort to fuse idealism, artistic form, the
high moral principle associated the genteel tradition
with culture, i.e. with the world of women. The
realm of men, i.e. of business, remained untrammeled
by its lofty notions and demands and could pursue its
down-to-earth, pragmatic course - less moral and
refined, but serviceable and immensely profitable.
With common sense practicality, the industrial tycoons
seem to have believed earnestly enough that the ends
justify the means. Their millions ensured employment,
material improvements, and cultural endowments which
amply atoned for whatever wrongs they committed in
the process of accumulating their wealth. The polarization of society worked to keep various social groups

and planes of thinking separate and thus, to tone down
contradictions and eliminate direct confrontations.
For better or worse, the genteel tradition confirmed
the "in-between" status of American intellectuals –
writers, artists and critics in particular.

The response of the literary circles to this
polarization appears paradoxical: writers seem not to
resent their relegation from the masculine sphere, but
fulfill their self-appointed mission with every
appearance of equanimity. As educators, they repeatedly
demonstrate possibilities and mutual advantages of
re-establishing order by means of overcoming the
fundamental split in American society. According to
the spirit of the age the novelist seldom arranges his
plots and characters for any direct or decisive
confrontation. The conventional system of rewards
and punishments serves as the main vehicle in pro-
nouncing judgment on fictional events and personal
merits. The latter are measured in three categories
as being those of a Christian (in the very broad
meaning, without any particular church affiliation),
a citizen, and a gentleman. The hierarchy of values
they promote belongs to the preceding century: they
seek to vindicate and instill in their readers norms,
virtues and standards of manners of the eighteenth
century gentry. A close analysis of children's
periodicals led Kelly to conclude:

> Successful socialization to the code
> of the gentleman made self-control of
> supreme importance. . . . Sensitivity
> to the need and rights of others
> complements self-control. Financial
> success and the so called employee
> virtues . . . are subordinated in the
> gentry's view to the development of
> character and self-control and the
> fostering of a willingness to serve
> society well.[21]

The model of an individual forwarded for general
emulation carried a considerable power of attraction.
Its major appeal, beside high social prestige, was
the image of a fully integrated personality. A
gentleman was a well-rounded person cultivated in body
and mind, whose pleasing appearance, winning manners,
and general savoir-faire reflect a corresponding
refinement of the spirit. Finding firm foundation
and support in rationality and self-discipline all

these qualities complement each other harmoniously.
The stress on cultivating personal virtues and talents
grew out of the central concept of social service.
Individual gifts and abilities should be usefully
employed for the benefit of the entire community;
they impose additional obligations on one's regular
duties to society, shared by everybody in equal
measure. The idea of public service, like that of
responsibility for general order and welfare, is
crucial to the gentry mode of thinking.

The gentry ideology proved as much a part of the
American heritage as the Constitution and democratic
government. Since the days of the Founding Fathers,
it suffered few modifications; certain particular
points which became obviously outdated had to be
adjusted to new conditions. The principal assumptions,
however, remained the same, losing but little relevance.
The fundamental emphasis on human perfectability and
inborn rationality, central to the concept of man in
the Age of Reason, ascribed special role to education,
without, however, making much distinction between
parental training, formal schooling or self-instruction.
More attention went to the harmonious development of
all faculties - body, spirit, and mind. In the context
of a recently established democracy, the gentility
code was not confined to a single class, although in
the early years of the republic the American landed
gentry, its main repository, set up the standards of
manners and ideas as well as the example of meeting
one's duties and responsibilities. Its code consisted
of clearly defined rules, principles and ideas that
anybody could learn and follow, thereby becoming a
gentleman in no way inferior to one born into the
station. In America the term gentleman defined neither
occupation nor family background but an ideology - a
set of beliefs and values to which he subscribed.

Carried into the nineteenth century the gentility
code proved adaptable to the emerging mercantile
capitalism which became the dominant ideology of the
more prosperous classes. Its impact upon education
in the 1830s and 1840s was decisive. Looking backward
on his childhood years from the point of view of the
early twentieth century, Henry Adams claimed that his
training - the concepts, assumptions, opinions, and
points of reference he was taught to share - belonged
essentially to the eighteenth century, not his own.
Nor was he the only one of his generation who found
his eighteenth century gentility inadequate in the

chaos of the post Civil War America.

In the course of the nineteenth century, the old
gentry class suffered a gradual decline: Stow Persons'
penetrating study of the problem analyses the growing
isolation of the old gentry in American society.

> In perfection of dress and manner,
> but even more in refinement of taste
> and delicacy of sentiment, the
> gentleman achieved the final
> realization of the form. By doing
> so he widened the gulf separating
> himself from the rough, vigorous
> industrial society of which he was,
> incongruously, a member. . . . It
> was the ultimate irony that a
> tradition that had always prided
> itself upon its masculinity should
> come to find itself best represented
> by its women.[22]

Once a dominant group in social and economic life,
after the Civil War the landed gentry was rapidly
losing control over national politics and business.
It continued its role as the intellectual and
society elite until the end of the century, but with
growing awareness of its own vulnerability and shrinking
influence. The centers of power were shifting to
other social groups; the new class of industrial and
financial magnates imitated the external features of
gentility without, however, sharing the values of
quality, order, and discipline. The initial effort
of the 1830s and 1840s to accommodate the
aggressiveness and mobility of the industrial system
through dissemination of democratic ideals and gentry
values became increasingly defensive after 1865.
Caught between a shrinking field of action and
diminished social significance on the one hand and
adherence to high culture and personal refinement
on the other, the tradition of gentility drifted
toward sentimentality, ineffectuality and decay of
the genteel. Thus, the expropriation of the gentry in
public life was, in fact, another aspect of a larger
and more complex process of which the economic disestablishment of women also formed a part. The
two operated simultaneously; actually they co-operated
in the disintegration of the existing social order.

> The second phase of the lady's trans-
> formation began with the nineteenth
> century separation of the gentry from
> the social-economic elite. . . . When
> the new gentry became separate from the
> rich and fashionable, the lady began
> the process of establishing her own
> identity as something more than a mere
> foil for the gentleman.[23]

Persons clearly perceives the polarization of society,
caused by joint processes altering the relative
position of the gentry class and of gentry women in
particular, as the influential factor in women's movement toward emancipation.

Much of the American writing published after the
Civil War bears the stamp of gentry ideology. The
intended as well as involuntary efforts to uphold
this tradition directed most attempts to redefine the
success ideal by shifting the emphasis from material
to spiritual gains. Some writers, first of all a
great many authors of self-help guidebooks as well
as Horatio Alger stories, were, as Richard Weiss
calls them, "nostalgic spokesmen of a dying order."[24]
Rex Burns uses a different term but actually means the
very same process which was altering American society.

> The self-help movement was in part an
> effort by mechanics whose yeomen dream
> was threatened by changing economic
> patterns but genteel spokesman also
> urged reclamation and expanded self-help
> in the business realm.[25]

After all, both groups, yeomen and gentry, belong to
the same agrarian mode of existence characteristic
for the early years of the United States. The
generation of Henry Adams and Howells was born into
the last vestiges of the old order but on reaching
maturity, found it gone beyond recall, replaced by
giant corporations, railroad empires, capital-labor
struggles and iniquities of public service.

Direct references to gentry standards, however,
appear rarely in the novels of the period. In The
Cliff-Dwellers (1893) Henry Fuller records a lengthy
discussion on the self-made and self-confident Chicago
society carried by several characters disturbed by its
shallow display and selfish indifference. The question

is "Why are things so horrible in this country?"

> Because there's no standard of manners -
> no resident country gentry to provide it.
> Our own rank country folks have never
> had such a check, and this horrible rout
> of foreign peasantry has just escaped
> from it.[26]

Fuller's explicit evocation of gentry standards seems
unique; usually the novelists stay content with
presenting them without actually naming their origin.
Thus, for example, Maurice Graham, the main hero in
Abigail Roe's Free, Yet Forging Their Own Chains
(1876), comments:

> Human nature is much the same in the
> palace and cot. We certainly cannot
> expect a higher standard of morality
> and self-restraint among the ignorant
> and undisciplined than we practice
> ourselves.[27]

A gentleman by training, although only a super-
intendent of coal mines by trade, Graham mentions
all the key virtues of true gentility - morality,
self-restraint, knowledge, and discipline, also the
responsibility of the educated and well-to-do to
set an example for the less fortunate. The prevailing
tone of novelistic preaching is, ordinarily, even more
vague; although the point made remains clear to the
simplest-minded, its social character and context are
generally obliterated.

> Then dimly there came to her [Julia's]
> mind a new sense of stewardship, and
> the use of her talents which would one
> day be required - not mere careless,
> free-handed charity, that costs no
> trouble or self-denial; but a seeking
> out of the truly deserving, and an
> effort to lighten somehow the weight
> of the world's suffering and destitution.[28]

The essentially negative attitude toward the
emancipation of women as well as the prevailing support
for the traditional family also seem traceable to the
gentry point of view. If so, the conventional
engagement or wedding ceremony closing fictional plots
functions on two levels at the same time. It rounds

157

off the romantic and sentimental adventures of the
young heroes in a neat and final manner. Ideologically,
their decision is charged with significance: upon
marriage the two "unattached" individuals become a
family, the basic unit of social organization and
order. Thus, they are integrated into the social
structure which they will reinforce and perpetuate in
turn.

The family model set for young couples, fictional
as well as real, recommends the traditional division
into masculine and feminine roles which, while
conplementary, are nevertheless mutually exclusive.
This tenacious adherence to the old patterns seems yet
another instance of the novelist's essentially defensive
attitude toward new tendencies in social customs. The
patriarchal family was dissolving rapidly under the
pressure of social forces reshaping American reality.
Richard Weiss claims that the tension between the
formal model of the family and the demands set by the
industrial system are reflected in the choice of
fictional characters. The frequent absence of the
father from the main scene of action, he argues, is
highly significant.

> The orphan was a convenient fictional
> figure in a society eager to accept
> change but uneasy about losing its
> past. Eliminating the father, a
> symbol of tradition and authority,
> made the acceptance of change possible
> without requiring an explicit
> rejection of tradition. Seen in this
> light, the orphan reflects the tension
> between stability and movement that is
> expressed so frequently in literature
> with success theme.[29]

In his History of Marriage and Family Willystine
Goodsell distinguished four factors which contributed
most to the disintegration of the old family structure:
the extension of the frontier into the wilderness of
the west, the rapid development of machine industry,
the powerful influence of liberalism and democratic
ideas, and finally the weakening of dogmatic
religion.

> . . . the knell of the patriarchal
> family was sounding even in the early
> decades of the new [nineteenth] century.

> Powerful social forces were at work
> sapping the ancient props of father
> power and reducing it to shadowy
> proportions.[30]

Thus, the new concept of marriage assigning ultimate
value to romantic love and personal happiness evolved
under the impact of forces operating for some forty
years. If economic disestablishment of women and
expropriation of the gentry form two major aspects of
socio-economic change, the emerging model of individualistic love-marriage reflects the parallel shift in
socio-cultural patterns. On all the three planes
actual accommodation to the demands of everyday life
precedes conscious realization or intellectual
reflection on its significance. It took a life-span
and the experience of a generation to cope pragmatically
with challenges and problems posed by new socio-economic
developments; another generation's life-time elapsed
before the extent, direction and consequences of change
became fully understood. American fiction of the last
quarter of the nineteenth century reflects this very
delay in comprehension: set in the American reality of
the 1870s and 1880s most novels of the period deal
with contemporaneous affairs and stay usually within
the limits of the probable. Their transgressions
against "realism," i.e. feasible representation of
the actual, result from too ardent a desire to
promote some worthy cause, or preach or criticize
numerous abuses and iniquities of the day. The
sentimental plot provides the central focus of
interest around which most novelists arrange their
description or discussion of current events.
Occasionally references to particular events can be
identified with fair accuracy - the New York streetcar
strike in 1888 described by Howells in A Hazard of
New Fortunes, the great Chicago fire in 1871 providing
dramatic scenery in E. P. Roe's Barriers Burned Away
or M. A. Foran's The Other Side. This topicality can
easily deceive a casual reader today as much as it did
a hundred years ago.

Every novelist's representation of reality is
unavoidably colored by his views, ideas, and attitudes.
In the case of American writers of the Gilded Age,
their interpretation of post-Civil War society appears
molded by the gentility code inherited from their
grandfathers, contemporaries of the Founding Fathers.
The succeeding generation of their fathers, born
already in the nineteenth century, cherished the old

norms and notions while acquiring the more pragmatic
skills of combining the demands of the practical
with those of the ideal in some tenable, if precarious
balance. Industrialization, expropriation of the
gentry, economic disestablishment of women, and
polarization of society appeared to them but ordinary
adversities and difficulties of individual life with
which they had to struggle. Only the next generation,
of the novelists writing in the 1870s and 1880s,
experienced these changes not as personal hardships
but as wide-scale social phenomena. Handed down a
mixed heritage of an old gentility code and the
practical experience of coping and accommodating to
the changing world, they were equipped to respond to
their contemporary reality on the intellectual as well
as pragmatic level. Hence, while ostensibly writing
about strikes, railroad corporations, divorce suits,
and society competition, they dealt - much more truly -
with much more complex consequences of social and
economic processes initiated in the first half of
the nineteenth century.

Among writers discussed here only Henry Adams and
Henry James definitely belonged to the former gentry
class by descent and family tradition. Others,
including the most talented and influencial Mark
Twain and W. D. Howells, moved up to the professional
class from humbler walks of life. Nevertheless, they
all identified with the gentry: adopting their
value system, their standards of manners and morals
these writers consciously reverted to the privileged
status of a social elite. Stow Persons goes as far as
to argue that "it became the principal function of
gentility in the nineteenth century to furnish the
social identity for those engaged in high cultural
activity."[31] The role of gentleman imposed the
obligation to conform to the norms prescribed by the
gentry code; at the same time it charged one with the
responsibility to elevate, direct, and control public
life so as to ensure its orderly and rational course.
The elite status of gentleman involves esteem as well
as duty: he is, as Julia Ward Howe, the leading
authority on true politeness insists, both a leader
and a guardian of social order.

> One of the great needs of society in
> all times is that its guardians shall
> take care that rules or institutions
> devised for some good end shall not
> become so perverted in the use made

> of them as to bring about the result
> most opposed to that which they were
> intended to secure.[32]

In the second half of the nineteenth century the task
as thus defined became virtually impossible. The former
prominence of the old gentry in American economy,
finance, commerce, and politics was diminishing
steadily for more than a quarter of the century. The
Civil War precipitated this decline indirectly so
that, by the 1870s, the remnants of this class found
themselves eliminated from public affairs, while
actual power in all areas shifted into the hands of
new monopolies.

> Along with the decline of democratic
> equality has come a different, though
> kindred, social change . . . equally
> undesirable - the transfer of social
> leadership from the professional to the
> commercial class. For her older
> personal ideal of the statesman or the
> lawyer, or the writer, industrial America
> has substituted that of a millionaire;
> the contemporary professional man or
> scholar is likely to be merely a satellite
> or agent of the commercial system.[33]

It may perhaps seem paradoxical that American
intellectuals and professionals adopted the moral
and behavioral code of a class which was rapidly
becoming marginal in public affairs. One would rather
expect the best informed and the most thoughtful group
in society to prove more enterprising, and attempt an
alliance with the progressive forces of the
industrial order. Such attempts were actually made:
the rise of national associations and professional
societies exerted powerful influence in curbing the
reckless and irresponsible acquisitiveness of the
robber barons. Howard Mumford Jones suggests that by
the 1890s the impact of professional opinion and
expertise was possibly more effective in modifying
business methods than all the denunciations by populists
and progressives.

> Expertise in social sciences and in
> psychology affected corporate
> management since specialists in
> economics, business practices, social
> psychology, and public relations were

161

> not so much telling management what it
> could do as telling management what it
> could not do. . . . . The development of
> professional societies in turn meant
> the development of informed professional
> opinion increasingly inaccessible to
> political and economic pressures and
> at the same time increasingly interested
> in national problems, national welfare,
> and predictive judgment.[34]

But the movement which helped to integrate scholars
and professionals into the mainstream of American
socio-economic life failed to accommodate artists and
writers. Once again, they were "left out" of the
active and productive sphere. Industrial, money-
oriented America appeared too preoccupied with
materialistic gains to care much for either art or
literature. On February 16, 1881, Henry James
commented on the fact in a letter to Thomas Sergent
Perry:

> You say that literature is going down
> in the U.S.A.. I quite agree with you -
> the stuff that is sent me seems to me
> written by eunuchs and seamstresses. . . .
> I suspect the age of letters is waning,
> for our time. It is the age of Panama
> Canals, of Sarah Bernhardt, of wheat-
> raising, of merely material expansion.
> Art, form may return but . . . - I
> don't believe they are eternal, as the
> poets say.[35]

Under such circumstances the social status and
function of a professional writer was not "given"
in America, in the sense of being an a priori
specified role to be assumed and enacted by an
individual. On the contrary. Whether aware of the
fact or not, American men of letters of the later
nineteenth century faced the necessity of "creating
social space" for themselves.

They resorted to the essentially eighteenth
century code of gentility because it provided what
they missed most in their own society - vindication
of aesthetic refinement, affirmation of the
intrinsic value of art and literature as well as
inherent nobility of cultural and intellectual pursuits.
As self-appointed heirs of the gentry class and gentry

162

tradition, they felt entitled to act as leaders, educators, and guardians of social order, i.e. to enter the role formerly played by the landed gentry. This alliance with the gentility code seldom resulted from a deliberate, fully realized act of choice; most writers of the period seem but half aware of the double motivation or purpose behind their work. The interest in the present - in the contemporary reality with its evils and abuses on the one hand and in popular and financial success of their books on the other - screens the underlying, often subconscious, uneasiness about one's real place in society.

The writer's essentially defensive attitude, reflected best in his persistent didacticism, betrays the precariousness of his social position. The effort to ingrain gentry values in popular concepts and to illustrate them in popular novels bears witness to the increasing awareness that the old norms and virtues were losing their relevance in the rapidly changing industrial and urban conditions. The very insistence on the didactic message seems to indicate that the novelists under discussion found it impossible to remain neutral in the confrontation with the new social issues. Their didacticism may be described, therefore, as a defensive tactic by means of which they sought to reaffirm the validity of gentry values. Vindicating and disseminating them, the novelists of the period strove to defend, uphold, and justify their own status as a social elite.

It is next to impossible to establish with any degree of precision or authority which comes first - the polarization of society which left American writers without a clearly defined position, or their alliance with the gentry tradition to which they were not heirs by birth. The two factors were, like other socio-economic phenomena referred to in this analysis (industrialization, expropriation of gentry, economic disestablishment of women), merely fragments of the complex process re-shaping America in the course of the nineteenth century. All these forces operated simultaneously, one change speeding and reinforcing the remaining ones.

Caught in a network of contradicting purposes and forces the writers had to define their own status, to make room for themselves and make themselves heard. Indeed, they were read and listened to by many. Jay Martin enumerates several factors which contributed most to creating steady demand for books.

> Technological improvements in bookmaking,
> the diffusion of education, innovations
> in merchandising, and the rising standard
> of living as well as the rising
> aspirations for culture - these all
> spilled over into the conditions of
> literary production.[36]

One may easily suppose, however, that the didactic
message of these books was accepted favorably as
often as it was ignored. Furnishing a rationale and
solution to the disturbing question of their social
function, the gentility code satisfied an immediate,
though for most, a subconscious need for affirmation
and security. Furthermore, it allowed them to fuse,
for better or worse, the two elements which but a
hundred years later appear absolutely incompatible -
realism and didacticism. The prevailing representation
of reality bears marks of both. Numerous novels of
the period describe poverty, corruption, foolishness
or sin truly enough, with an evident purpose that
these wrongs, whether personal or social, may be
corrected. They deal with the usual and the probable
world which, naturally enough, is narrowed down to
the respectable and genteel to promote desirable
behavioral patterns. The negative and positive sides
of their view of contemporary existence complement
each other to emphasize the author's message.

The educational purpose which in the hands of
William Dean Howells, the chief promoter of realism
in American fiction, refrained from any direct or
externally imposed moralizing, was based, according to
Everett Carter, on three assumptions.

> . . . That life, social life as lived
> in the world Howells knew, was valuable,
> and was permeated with morality; that
> its continued health depended upon the
> use of human reason to overcome the
> anarchic selfishness of human passions;
> that an objective portrayal of human
> life, by art, will illustrate the
> superior value of social, civilized
> man, of human reason over animal
> passion and primitive ignorance.[37]

164

Hence, he concludes, to fulfill this goal the novel
imitated life but did it selectively.

> . . . if a novel was to tell the truth
> about life, it would have to mimic a
> world in which the supremacy of such
> '[i.e. unreasonable, ungoverned] passions
> was punished by human unhappiness.[38]

Aiming to counteract the general sense of confusion
dominating everyday experience the novelists of the
two decades offered a singular, carefully adjusted
interpretation of the contemporaneous reality.
A great many facts, problems, affairs and details of
daily life are faithfully transferred from direct
experience into fictional tales. Numerous discrepancies between the novelistic version and our more
sober, documented knowledge of the era occurred first
of all through the process of conscious selection
of material. Such elements that would contradict
the acceptable image of the world, or would offend
the reader's sensibility, were either modified, toned
down or, most frequently, left out of the picture.
In doing so, the authors wished to combine their
vision of what life was with what it, from their point
of view, should have been.

Applying here the definition of Lawrence D.
Wieder, we can assume that most novelists of the
later nineteenth century employed, consciously or
not, gentility as a normative code.

> A normative code consists of a collection
> of embedded instructions for perception.
> While these instructions are about the
> organization [of society], they are also
> a feature or aspect of that same
> organization.[39]

The actual human experience as well as the moral
principle enclosed in the fictional story constituted
tangible, recognizable components of the contemporary
social reality; most readers responded to them with a
sense of familiarity or commonly shared knowledge. At
the same time, both these elements were employed as
tools for interpretation of this very reality. In
other words, they served as a norm as well as a formula
for description; moreover, they functioned in feedback.

165

Notes

1. George Santayana, "Genteel Tradition in American Philosophy," in Genteel Tradition (Cambridge, Mass., 1967), p. 40.

2. H. H. Boyesen, "Why We Have No Great Novelists," The Forum, February 1887, p. 619.

3, W. D. Howells, A Hazard of New Fortunes (New York, 1965), p. 123.

4. Cf. Howells, "The Man of Letters as a Man of Business;" "That man of letters must make up his mind that in the United States the fate of the book is in the hands of the women. It is the women with us who have the most leisure, and they read the most books. They are far better educated, for the most part, than our men, and their tastes, if not their minds, are more cultivated. Our men read the newspapers, but our women read the books; the more refined among them read the magazines." Quoted after L. T. Goldman, "A Different View of the Iron Madonna: William Dean Howells and His Magazine Audience," The New England Quarterly, December 1977, p. 577.

5. Gerald Garson, Polite Americans (New York, 1966), p. 187.

6. For the detailed analysis of this alliance see Ann Douglas, The Feminization of American Culture (New York, 1977).

7. This is not to say that New England lost its intellectual vitality. If it suffered a slight decline on the economic plane, as the crucial industrial centers moved away, mainly to the west, and many towns and villages dwindled to stagnation, its leadership in other areas continued unchanged - in finance and politics, and even in a larger measure in professions, science, education, and the arts. Culturally and intellectually New England remained the most lively and influential region of the U.S.

8. Everett Carter, Howells and The Age of Realism.

9. Henry Adams, The Education of Henry Adams (New York, 1931), p. 33.

10. Howells, <u>A Hazard of New Fortunes</u>, p. 423.

11. Carter, p. 50.

12. Foran, <u>The Other Side</u> (Washington, 1886), p. 424.
    Foran's presentation of Mary Marmane, a minor
    character, is an excellent example of a stereotyped
    characterization. The passage runs as follows:
    "Still in girlhood she was a wild, romping, happy,
    blooming child of nature . . . fond of roaming
    the wide fields . . . and plucking wild
    flowers; . . . As she grew older, she assumed
    household duties - could bake, cook or churn
    butter . . . , was a capital seamstress - . . .
    and sometimes helped her father by keeping his
    accounts - in a word she was never idle or
    unemployed; and yet amidst all these duties she
    found time to read and study and become pretty
    well versed in all the needful modern arts and
    sciences." Foran's description of his hero is
    as superlative: " . . . now he stood before these
    people in dark pants, and a tight-fitting cotton
    shirt, which adhered so closely to his person
    as to resemble the drapery . . . ; the corded
    muscles of his chest, neck and arms standing out
    in bold relief like the ridges of marble . . .
    he stood there, a man of brawn, muscle and
    virility, the embodiment of masculine power,
    force, courage, and physical stamina, each and
    all of which attributes claim the admiration of
    woman and exact her love," p. 170.

13. W. T. Ihamon, Jr., "Horatio Alger and American
    Modernism: the One-Dimensional Social Formula,"
    <u>American Studies</u>, Fall 1976, Vol. XVII, No. 2,
    p. 12.

14. <u>Ibid</u>.

15. Cf. John Tebbel, <u>From Rags to Riches</u> (New York,
    1963), p. 11. " . . . Alger was not a best
    selling author in his lifetime, with a single
    exception. At the time of his death, his total
    sales were not more than 800,000, a respectable
    figure but hardly to be compared with those of
    real best-selling writers. . . . The big Alger
    sales did not come until the paperback
    publishers began to take him up after his
    death, first in twenty-five cents editions
    and finally in the dime novel format. Alger

enthusiasts have departed so far from reality
as to estimate his total sales as high as
three hundred million, a figure not to be
taken seriously. . . . Mott estimates the
total at no more than 16 or 17 million, an
estimate in which other experts concur."

16. R. Gordon Kelly, Mother Was a Lady (Westport,
     Conn., 1974), p. 35.

17. E. C. Kirkland, Dream and Thought in Business
     Community, 1860-1900 (Ithaca, N.Y., 1956), p. 7.

18. Cf. Henry James' well known list of American
     deficiencies: "No state in the European sense
     of the word, and indeed barely a specific national
     name. No sovereign, no court, no personal
     loyalty, no aristocracy, no church, no clergy,
     no army, no diplomatic service, no country
     gentlemen, no palaces, no castles, nor manors,
     nor country houses, nor parsonages, nor
     thatched cottages, nor ivied ruins; no
     cathedrals, nor abbeys, nor little Norman
     churches; no great universities nor public
     schools - no Oxford nor Eton, nor Harrow; no
     literature, no novels, no museums, no pictures,
     no political society . . ."

19. John Higham, "Integrating America: The Problem
     of Assimilation in the Nineteenth Century," a
     paper read at the Third Conference of Polish
     and American Historians, Poznan, May 1979.

20. H. M. Jones, The Age of Energy (New York, 1970),
     pp. 216, 233, 237.

21. Kelly, p. 74.

22. Stow Persons, The Decline of American
     Gentility (New York, 1973), pp. 273, 275.

23. Ibid., p. 82.

24. Richard Weiss, American Myth of Success (New
     York, 1969), p. 49.

25. Rex Burns, Success in America (Amherst, Mass.,
     1976), p. 74.

26. Henry Fuller, The Cliff-Dwellers (New York,

1893), p. 236.

. Abigail Roe, _Free, Yet Forging Their Own Chains_
    (New York, 1876), p. 97.

28. _Ibid._, p. 122.

29. Weis, p. 58.

30. Willystine Goodsell, _A History of Marriage and
     Family_ (New York, 1934), p. 457.

31. Persons, p. 55.

32. J. W. Howe, _Is Polite Society Polite?_ (Boston,
     1895), p. 116.

33. W. F. Taylor, _The Economic Novel in America_
     (New York, 1973), p. 255.

34. Jones, p. 175.

35. T. T. S. Perry, February 16, 1881. _Letters
     1875-1883_ (Cambridge, Mass., 1975), II, p. 341.

36. Jay Martin, _The Harvests of Change_ (Englewood
     Cliffs, N.J., 1967), p. 19.

37. Carter, p. 157.

38. _Ibid._, p. 163.

39. L. D. Wieder, _Language and Social Reality_ (The
     Hague, 1974), p. 203.

Afterword

The novelists discussed here form a separate social group primarily because they subscribe to a definite set of norms and values. The instrumental use to which they put the gentility code carries, I believe, additional significance. It served them as a tool to interpret reality, i.e. to impose a comprehensible order upon the external world of their times. By doing so they sought to establish some intellectual and emotional control over their bewildering and chaotic existence. It is highly ironic that their efforts to understand contemporary industrial and urban America placed them in the rearguard of their society. Only in the 1890s could the younger generation, among whom Crane and Norris were, perhaps, the most talented, shift to new currents of thought, new concepts and attitudes. The turning point comes after 1900 - with Theodore Dreiser, Upton Sinclair, Jack London, Sherwood Anderson, Gertrude Stein, Sinclair Lewis and their juniors. However they differ in their respective philosophical views or creeds, they no longer believe the world to be moral or rational. For better or worse they accept that the universe is amoral, basically indifferent, though sometimes hostile, to human beings and their efforts. A novelist can observe human struggles with the cool detachment of a scientist or celebrate the ceaseless, irresistible workings of elemental forces - but any judgment is essentially presumptuous. Those who held to the old views and values were left far behind, like Howells who outlived his influence, his audience, even his reputation. Among such as him, few were as articulate as Henry Adams.

> The Trusts and Corporations . . . that had been created since 1840 . . . were obnoxious because of their vigorous and unscrupulous energy. They were revolutionary, troubling all the old conventions and values. . . . They tore society to pieces and trampled it under foot. As one of their earliest victims, a citizen of Quincy, born in 1838, had learned submission and silence, for he knew that, under the laws of mechanics, any change . . . must make his situation only worse. . . . The new man could

170

be only a child born of contact between
the new and the old energies.[1]

---

[1]Henry Adams, The Education of Henry Adams (New
York, 1931), p. 500.